Patient's Healthcare Portfolio

Patient's Healthcare Portfolio
A Practitioner's Guide to
Providing Tools for Patients

by

Rebecca Mendoza Saltiel Busch

CRC Press
Taylor & Francis Group
Boca Raton London New York

CRC Press is an imprint of the
Taylor & Francis Group, an **informa** business

A PRODUCTIVITY PRESS BOOK

CRC Press
Taylor & Francis Group
6000 Broken Sound Parkway NW, Suite 300
Boca Raton, FL 33487-2742

First issued in paperback 2019

© 2017 by Rebecca Mendoza Saltiel Busch
CRC Press is an imprint of Taylor & Francis Group, an Informa business

No claim to original U.S. Government works

ISBN-13: 978-1-4987-7602-8 (pbk)

Library of Congress Cataloging-in-Publication Data

Names: Busch, Rebecca S., author.
Title: Patient's healthcare portfolio : a practitioner's guide to providing tools for patients / Rebecca Mendoza Saltiel Busch.
Description: Boca Raton : Taylor & Francis, 2017.
Identifiers: LCCN 2016039381| ISBN 9781498776028 (pbk. : alk. paper) | ISBN 9781498776035 (eBook)
Subjects: | MESH: Health Information Management | Health Records, Personal | Patient Advocacy | Guideline
Classification: LCC R858.A2 | NLM W X 173 | DDC 362.10285--dc23
LC record available at https://lccn.loc.gov/2016039381

Visit the Taylor & Francis Web site at
http://www.taylorandfrancis.com

and the CRC Press Web site at
http://www.crcpress.com

To the amazing women who have inspired so many

Francisca Aida Mendoza Saltiel

Maria Dolores Mendoza Perez

Gregoria Garcia Mendoza

Rebecca Levy Saltiel

Contents

SECTION III   PATIENT ADVOCACY PHP TEMPLATES

Preface

"Persons attempting to find a motive in this narrative will be prosecuted; persons attempting to find a moral in it will be banished; persons attempting to find a plot in it will be shot.
    BY ORDER OF THE AUTHOR per
    G.G., CHIEF OF ORDNANCE"

Mark Twain
The Adventures of Huckleberry Finn

The goal in creating this book is to share critical insider information with industry stakeholders and healthcare consumers at large, primarily caregivers and patients. One of this book's principal objectives is to better equip and prepare healthcare advocates and their consumers with the knowledge, skills, abilities, and tools to obtain the best care possible and simplify the convoluted financial and legal issues associated with America's overwhelming healthcare system. Another principal objective of this book is to guide and assist patient advocates to provide comprehensive, simple, common language answers to their clients' healthcare questions. Patient advocates will most likely find themselves on healthcare's frontline as educators, navigators, and information mediators, and must be prepared to act in that role.

The backdrop to this book is experiences gained through my company, Medical Business Associates. Medical Business Associates, Inc. (MBA) was formed in 1991 with the vision of delivering medical data audit, architecture, and analytic support services to healthcare providers, payers, government agencies, employers and ultimately, patients. MBA's 25-year legacy working in the health data industry affords a comprehensive understanding of America's healthcare delivery system. It has also provided a unique and valuable insight into the innumerable problems, issues, and risks that patients face when they require medical care.

Patient's Healthcare Portfolio: A Practitioner's Guide to Providing Tools for Patients is organized into three sections. Section I documents a series of instructor guidance notes. Notwithstanding our current health industries' rapidly evolving technology, patient advocacy at its core is a person-to-person matter. Practice guides are included that emphasize the need to first understand our patient as a person before the eventual deep dive into their pressing health issues.

Section II contains fundamental material critical for advocates and their patients to understand in order to effectively translate complicated issues or problems into a simplified, actionable path forward. Included are a number of typical scenarios that MBA routinely encounter during patient advocacy interaction. These events posed significant barriers to patients navigating their healthcare. Patient advocates must rely on their knowledge and experience to effectively educate patients attempting to navigate America's overwhelming and multifaceted healthcare system.

Section III contains a series of templates for creating a personal healthcare portfolio. These templates will facilitate a more accurate and retrievable set of critical patient (personal) health records that are retained by providers (doctors and hospitals). Additional templates are provided that serve as illustrative examples on how to obtain a patient's personal health information from providers and/or payers.

MBA continues to work with individuals who find that they are lost, stuck, or in some cases harmed by our present healthcare system. The ultimate goal is to empower our patients to fully comprehend, appreciate, and begin to self-advocate for their personal healthcare. Moreover, patient advocates are a great resource for patients who need a bit of extra support, direction, and coaching, or for family members or caregivers who become overwhelmed by the stress of taking care of a friend or family member.

This book was developed to share the means and methods we have discovered that most effectively enable patients and advocates to take charge of their healthcare affairs and/or better assist those who, for whatever reason, desperately need your help.

Acknowledgments

The acknowledgement of a single possibility can change everything.

Aberjhani
Splendid Literarium: A Treasury of Stories,
Aphorisms, Poems, and Essays

When thinking of patient advocacy, all roads lead directly to my father, Dr. Alberto Saltiel, a family practitioner, surgeon, and *the* ultimate patient advocate. There are countless stories, encounters, and personal observations of how my father assisted patients in getting the proper care they needed. I recall a local newspaper story of a patient who, when hearing that my father was retiring the obstetrician portion of his practice, got pregnant and flew from California to Chicago just to make sure that he delivered her first born. On the day he retired from delivering babies, he received an indescribable standing ovation from the nursing staff at MacNeal Memorial Hospital. I will never forget the looks of awe and respect he received from his peers and the calming reassurance he provided to patients when discussing everything from matters of life and death to simple conversations concerning family and friends. My father's work left a permanent impression on everyone he touched and provided me the self-confidence to recognize what is right and simply *just wrong* in how patient care is managed.

My father often tells stories about representatives from both public and private insurance companies who would inquire about his success in basic fundamental patient care. Nurses from the Medicaid program were particularly curious as to why his mothers and babies had such low complication rates. Simple: patient education—the root of well-being in making informed decisions.

The answer: Patient education. One reason so many patients fall through the cracks is a failure by providers and plan sponsors to teach them how to avoid being misguided, mistreated, or otherwise short-changed by the healthcare system.

Lesson learned from my father: Providers and plan sponsors *must* make time to educate their patients on options for a healthy life and *must* inform patients of their rights.

My mother: A penchant for advocacy and teaching comes from my mom, Francis Aida Mendoza Saltiel—a school teacher, passionate mother, and a mentor of many life lessons.

Lesson learned from my mother: We are educators of youth and our peers. Compassion and knowledge transfer is critical to the health and welfare of family.

The combined ethical values and passions bestowed on me by my parents to help those in need are not only my treasured inheritance, but also my constant motivation for being a health advocate.

Author

I've got the key to my castle in the air, but whether I can unlock the door remains to be seen.

Louisa May Alcott
Little Women

Rebecca Mendoza Saltiel Busch is a registered nurse, patient advocate, data scientist, and healthcare consultant. Rebecca is the founder and chief executive officer of Medical Business Associates, Inc. (MBA), established in 1991 as a minority, woman-owned medical data auditing and healthcare consulting firm. As a registered nurse in an acute care setting, she saw firsthand how data inundate the healthcare environment. For her clients, the devil is always in the detail—the data. In 2015, we saw the emergence of a big data revolution in healthcare that is driving health industry organizations to develop holistic policies to provide patients access to their medical information while simultaneously protecting it.

Rebecca has been an advocate for patients who have found themselves trapped, lost, and hurt by our healthcare system. Her goals are to innovate solutions, effect change, and "pay it forward." Rebecca donates a significant portion of time to helping patients overcome the many obstacles that insurance carriers and healthcare providers—to name a few—incorporate into their business models to misrepresent, overcharge, or delay or deny patients from getting proper access to medical care. Rebecca's mission, and one of MBA's many charters, is consumer healthcare education that provides clients the knowledge, skills, and abilities to be their own best advocate. Rebecca's experiences in helping patients navigate the healthcare maze compelled her to write this book as a practical patient advocate guide to avoid the many pitfalls and ethically challenged predators loitering in our current healthcare system. This book will help patients and give future patient advocates the ability to identify, collect, and organize the information necessary to make the best decisions concerning their own healthcare.

As the daughter of a physician and a teacher, she can't help but be drawn toward paying it forward—this book is dedicated to providing professionals a framework to aid in the mission of empowering others to be their own best advocate.

Academic Background

An accomplished author, educator, and business developer, Rebecca has written over 52 articles and made more than 200 presentations to consumers, government agencies, and corporate and professional entities. She has published four books and contributed to material published by a number of other authors. These include

- *Leveraging Data in Healthcare*: *Best Practices for Controlling, Analyzing, and Using Data* by Rebecca Busch, HIMSS—CRC Press December 2015
- *Case Studies in Insurance Fraud* by Joseph T. Wells (editor) "Ignorance is Bliss, While it Lasts" a case study on insurance fraud by Rebecca Busch (contributing author) John Wiley & Sons, Inc., June 2013, Chapter 25. *Healthcare Fraud*: *Audit & Detection Guidebook* by Rebecca Saltiel Busch (author), Wiley & Sons Publications, June 2012 (2nd Edition)
- *Personal Healthcare Portfolio*: *Your Health & Wellness Record* by Rebecca Saltiel Busch, Medical Business Associates, Inc., June 2010.
- *Legal Nurse Consulting*: *Principles and Practices, Third Edition* edited by Anne Peterson and Lynda Kopishke, Chapter 12 pp. 251–272 "Government-Sponsored Healthcare Plans and General Case Evaluations," AALNC CRC Press, February 2010.
- *Electronic Health Records*: *An Audit and Internal Control Guide* by Rebecca S. Busch, John Wiley & Sons, Inc., July 2008.
- *Case Studies in Computer Fraud*: *The Bytes that Bite* by Joseph T. Wells (editor) "I Do" a case study on identity theft by Rebecca Busch (contributing author) John Wiley & Sons, Inc., August 2008.
- *Healthcare Fraud*: *Audit & Detection Guidebook* by Rebecca Busch (author), Wiley & Sons Publications, October 2007.
- *Fraud Casebook*: *Lessons from the Bad Side of Business* Joseph T. Wells (editor), Chapter 59 "Bodies for Rent" by Rebecca Busch, John Wiley & Sons Publications, July 2007.

Rebecca Mendoza Saltiel Busch, RN, MBA, CCM, CFE, CPC, CHS-III, CRMA, CICA, FIALCP, FHFMA has been granted U.S. data analytic design patent with pharmaceutical applications; one U.S. patent pertaining to electronic health record case management systems; and other patents pending on an anomaly tracking system and an interactive, iterative behavioral model, system and method for detecting fraud, waste, and abuse. She is also an adjunct professor within a masters certificate program for healthcare fraud, risk management, and compliance program at Florida Atlantic University, and a faculty member of the Association of Certified Fraud Examiners.

Chapter 1

Patient Advocate Defined

Be an advocate for the people and causes important to you, using the most powerful tool only you have—your personal stories.

John Capecci and Timothy Cage
Living Proof: Your Story to Make a Difference

Patients are getting lost, confused, and frustrated, and are losing confidence in receiving the right healthcare support when they need it. The evolving role of a patient advocate as a navigator, storyteller, infomediary specialist, and educator is in great demand. Simply stated, the patient advocate seeks to inform and empower the patient to take control of their healthcare. The healthcare transformational goal is to first recognize the current health data readiness state, followed by a plan to evolve, validate, and become a data-driven consumer.

To be an effective patient advocate, one needs to learn how to direct, inform, and educate the patient. Generally, the advocate has the capacity to take notes on behalf of the patient, understand issues, ask questions, and be able to relay information to coordinate the required care and resources. That is to say, the patient advocate becomes a second set of eyes and ears. A certain knowledge is required to help the patient get the right information, at the right time, to make the right healthcare decision.

Depending on the level of care a patient requires, an advocate such as an attorney, friend, nurse, ombudsman, physician, or social worker with professional experience may be of assistance in supporting a patient's rights. These may include matters such as the right to access a healthcare provider, the right to obtain confidential care, and the right of the patient to work after diagnosis or treatment. Acting as a liaison, the advocate helps a patient coordinate various healthcare players, including doctors, insurance companies, employers, case managers, lawyers, and others selected by the patient. An advocate's professional expertise may help resolve issues concerning medical bills, understanding the complexities of diagnosis codes, and dealing with job discrimination related to health issues. Every patient has different circumstances, preferences, and beliefs, informed advocates can provide alternative options regarding doctors' orders while keeping the patient's best interests in mind.

> **Family Advocate Experience:** A nephew describes the experience of taking on the role of an advocate for an elderly aunt. In this role, his greatest frustration involved making sure that all her providers had the same information. He actually maintained a complete set of records and brought it with him. He recalls driving his aunt to an elective surgery. During preop, the nurse came out and informed the family that the electronic medical record system had crashed and lost all of the aunt's healthcare records. She was prepped and ready to go to surgery. He tells the story of how he pulled out his briefcase and handed the nurse a complete history of his aunt and the copies of records he had obtained from that provider prior to their system crashing. The family advocate in this scenario was prepared by having all of the aunt's pertinent health information.
> **Lesson Learned:** Have independent access and copies of your electronic health records.

Patient discussion points on patient advocacy: What does a patient advocate do?

- Act as a sounding board to formulate intelligent decisions
- Have the ability to gather all financial and clinical records
- Coordinate ongoing care or obtain access to care
- Accompany patients to medical appointments to help them understand information relayed by the provider
- Facilitate the resolution of conflicts, confusion, or general lack of information
- Facilitate the creation of a personal health record or portfolio
- Check in with the patient and caregivers periodically to ensure issues/concerns do not fall through the cracks
- Ensure that providers are sharing information to and from the entire team
- Have a professional or formal relationship with the patient
- Act as a contractor to facilitate a specific patient or family need
- Provide training to patients and family members on practices that most effectively manage and resource patient care
- Coordinate multiple providers and their records for those patients with chronic conditions
- Remind patients of the option to seek alternative opinions
- Defer to the patient for all final decisions
- Assist patients to be their own advocate by utilizing these skill sets
- Encourage family members to act as an advocate and/or provide patient care

Also, consider the advantages of a professional or experienced patient advocate who is knowledgeable in healthcare networking environments. Being informed about the most superlative practices is crucial in today's healthcare environment. Another vital aspect is the ability to educate patients on the perils of fraud, waste, and abuse (FWA).

Patient discussion points on FWA activities may include:

■ Medical errors
■ Financial errors
■ Medical identity theft
■ Counterfeit prescription medications
■ Medically unnecessary services
■ Denial of entitled services
■ Other deceptive or misleading activities by healthcare providers, payers, insurers, and others

The following are some tools and services to assist advocates and patients in taking control of their healthcare, with the hopeful intent of eliminating the besieged feeling many receive from its navigation.

Patient discussion points on tools and services: What are the tools and services that can help manage your healthcare?

Patient discussion points on tools may include:

■ Personal healthcare record (PHR) management tools:
  – Illustrative example provided by Medical Business Associates, Inc. (MBA).
    • **Personal healthcare portfolio** (paper-based PHR)
    • **PortFolia** (software-based PHR)
    • **ePortFolia** (web-based PHR)
  – The American Health Information Management Association (AHIMA.org) provides a listing of other PHR tools.

■ Patient hotline
■ Patient coaching
■ Patient education seminars, webinars, and workshops
■ Medical bill review
■ Clinical case management services
■ Financial case management services
■ Patient advocate training and workshops
  – Commercial offerings that provide health adviser-type "tools" to seek affordable healthcare support

Patient Advocate Experience: A patient obtained a copy of their medical records. One of those records included paperwork from an emergency room admission. Upon review, the electronic patient consent form that was signed but not read at the time included specific contractual language regarding payment terms that was never actually explained to the patient. Of particular concern was the statement "the patient provides consent to pull credit reports and obtain personal financial information by the provider and their representatives." The patient was instructed that it is their right to revoke consent for access to credit reports and personal financial records. The letter was sent registered to the provider.

Lesson Learned: Read, request copies, and understand what you are asked to sign.

When seeking an advocate, understand their specific area of expertise and focus.

Some may be focused on the financial side of healthcare, others in the clinical, special education, disability, and/or behavioral health segments. The advocate should be an expert in helping people understand how money and information function in healthcare. Having the right data at the right time will help people make intelligent health and financial decisions.

Whether patient advocates provide fraud prevention and detection, auditing, consulting and training services, or general support to navigate the medical minefield of information, they ultimately strive to empower patients in the management of their own healthcare.

Chapter 2

Personal Healthcare Portfolio Model Defined

You can have data without information, but you cannot have information without data.

Daniel Keys Moran
Computer Programmer and Science Fiction Writer

As a Model

The personal healthcare portfolio (PHP) model is a patient-centric health data management guide and tool used by providers, advocates, and most importantly—patients. The PHP portfolio model highlighted in Section III identifies and describes critical data elements contained within standardized topic frameworks on how these critical data elements relate or in fact must relate to each other. The critical topic frameworks and related templates are segmented into **health**, **wellness management**, **financial**, and **personal health assessments**. The PHP model provides a practical illustration of how to create, manage, validate, and update patient-centric (most critical) health information in a meaningful way to facilitate and ensure an individual's defined health objectives are met.

   PHP model strategic objectives:

- Aggregate, capture, and document critical data points that significantly increase and or ensure the individual's ability to
    - Self-advocate in a meaningful, productive way
    - Make the best informed healthcare decision(s)
    - Select the right resources at the right time
    - Avoid adverse health events

- Manage ongoing health
- Manage healthcare costs
- Avoid adverse financial events
- Build self-confidence
- Maximize patient/provider integration and understanding
- Self-advocate in a meaningful, productive way

Data Management Capability

Data management (among organizations) as a scientifically based discipline is evolving in form and pace among and within various industries. Often missing in the equation of a data management plan is the capacity of an organization to effectuate the management of their data. Does the organization have the capacity to manage data? The same could be said about the individuals within that organization. Do they have the capacity to manage the data within the respective professional disciplines? In preparing to address this question of capacity to measure, the model presented in this chapter germinated from the study of the **DATA MANAGEMENT CAPABILITY ASSESSMENT MODEL** (DCAM).* The DCAM was created collaboratively by members of the Enterprise Data Management (EDM) Council—a trade association that focuses on data management standards and best practices. Together with their membership, which comprises over 190 major investment banks, buy-side/sell-side firms, vendors, market data companies, and regulatory bodies, the EDM Council developed the DCAM as a standard criterion for measuring data management capacity. The DCAM focuses on a set of criteria that identifies and measures the capabilities needed to develop and sustain an effective data management program. Although originally introduced into the banking industry, the concept of managing information via a set of standard capabilities is gaining value across industries. For the patient advocate, leveraging these concepts can serve as a reference point in developing the need to have a model and tool to assess a patient's capability and sustainability in managing their own healthcare data.

Introduction to Patient-Centric Health Data Management Strategy

Used as a noun, the word *data* simply implies information, static numbers, words, or symbols that blandly stare back as us as if we were looking at an old photo. Looking at the words *data or information* from a different perspective, that of an action verb, this same stagnant information morphs and mobilizes through processes of identification, coordination, and integration of acquired data

---

* http://www.edmcouncil.org/dcam.

sets that maximize patient/provider insight. The key is, "you don't know what you don't know … it is there, so find it, validate it and put it to use!" From the patient's perspective, the strategy is to utilize the PHP model to obtain, consolidate, organize, and process all personal health information to achieve a full accounting of your medical or health status. Comprehensiveness and quality of a patient's personal health information are directly proportional to the quality, integrity, and timeliness of care provided. Prompt, focused, correct … in some cases your healthcare may define your life's immediate path forward and "time can be of the essence." That is not the time to begin a search to consolidate a lifetime's worth of medical or health records scattered across the landscape.

PHP: Health Data Management Strategy

PHP's health data management strategy defines the purpose of the health data management program in a way that is meaningful to patients and stakeholders who are identified by patients, advocates, and providers.

PHP: Patient Capability Assessment Model

The patient capability assessment model provides patient advocates a mechanism to assess patient readiness to better manage their own health data. Patients simply cannot begin to advocate on their own behalf if they are not engaged. Patient engagement is defined by the degree of health data management-centricity accepted and controlled by patients. Patient engagement in this model is defined on a continuum. Of note, one of the first roles and responsibilities of the patient advocate must be to assess a patient's current capability to advocate on his or her own behalf. The patient's capability score (see Table 2.1) should parallel the advocate's action plan when working with the individual.

Assessing an individual's knowledge, skills, ability, and readiness to receive, manage, and assimilate their personal health information can be as complex as learning to navigate the overall healthcare system itself. A patient advocate must first establish a gap assessment tool (Table 2.1) to develop the most thorough understanding of the patient's current capabilities or the degree to which they can effectively and responsibly self-manage their personal health information. The advocate may start by creating a data workflow chart of how the patient currently interacts with the healthcare system, in addition to a detailed inventory of all healthcare stakeholders involved in episodes of care (anyone that influences, touches, or directs care). For example, if the patient has an active health plan or coverage, are they making healthcare choices based on plan provisions or on what they really require medically? Does the advocate understand how to define and evaluate what the health plan is actually covering (who, what, where, when, how many, costs, if this-if-that network, etc.), and when and how these services

Table 2.1 HDMS Patient Data Readiness (Score) Categories

Score	Category	Description	Characteristics	Advocate Checklist
1	Not initiated	No planning performed	No formal listing of healthcare providers; unclear on current health and wellness status; has not initiated health data collection procedures. Individual is unclear on how to use their health plan provisions and has no clear understanding of planning basic or specific provisions. Individual is unclear whether or when to seek healthcare assistance or wellness support.	Minimum—basic information about • Healthcare stakeholders: providers of care, any health plan (employer based, government, or private) • Healthcare information: PHI or medical identity
2	Conceptual	Initial planning stages	Initial collection and an organized list of current providers; acquires an informal listing of health and care history; is aware of all current treatment regimens. Is reactive to current healthcare plan provisions. Does not necessarily seek services outside of their health plan.	Information about healthcare; basic knowledge about healthcare plans; knowledge of specific stakeholder and health information.
3	Developmental	Engagement underway	Has collected and organized the current provider list; has a formal listing of known history; has documented and updated all current and ongoing treatment regimens. Understands where to locate health plan provisions and seek approval for healthcare services.	Information about providers' medical record history. Initiates collection of stakeholder and health information.

Table 2.1 (*Continued*)   HDMS Patient Data Readiness (Score) Categories

Score	Category	Description	Characteristics	Advocate Checklist
4	Defined	Concept of operations (plan) defined and verified	Has collected and organized the current providers, including a complete listing of demographic information; history of payment activity; coverage activity by all policies; formal listing of known health history; documented and updated history of current and ongoing treatment regimens. Interacts with healthcare plan administration; understands mechanism to select healthcare plans based on offerings in relation to personal needs.	Detailed information of providers; detailed information of plans; detailed medical history; detailed payment history.
5	Achieved	Adopted and utilized	Has collected and organized current providers with a comprehensive listing of demographic information; history of payment activity; coverage activity of all policies, including supporting documentation; documented formal list of known health history; documented and updated all current and ongoing treatment regimens and supporting documentation. Has demonstrated a process and/or selection of tools to manage the process. Understands options for pursuing resource gaps in health plan provisions.	Independently manage the process; perpetual methodology; defined tools for ongoing updates.

(Continued)

Table 2.1 (*Continued*) HDMS Patient Data Readiness (Score) Categories

Score	Category	Description	Characteristics	Advocate Checklist
6	Enhanced	Integrated	Has achieved the foregoing attributes and demonstrates the actions of a health data-driven consumer. Understands how to navigate and pursue options in resource, service, and product gaps within health plan provisions. Articulates options to mediate denials of services; reviews and understands healthcare financial implications. Understands how to seek assistance when encumbered with the process.	Data-driven consumer.

are delivered or not? Beware—from the patient's perspective (health plan or not), they will seek healthcare services when a particular need arises, and so the task begins.

PHP Practice Principals

The following practice principals define a starting point within our patient advocacy industry that establishes metrics and measurements that benchmark patient data readiness assessments. Patient advocates should assess patient engagement gaps and facilitate a plan(s) that guides the patient to effectively manage/comanage their own health information.

1. **Health Data Management Strategy**
   a. Health data management strategy (HDMS) needs must be documented in collaboration with the patient, identified stakeholders, resources, and technology utilization.
   b. Objectives must be identified and agreed upon by the individual.
      i. All third-party support to patients will be identified
      ii. The currency of the third-party patient support is identified
   c. The individual has the resources and mechanisms to achieve the objectives.

d. All objectives are incorporated in the healthcare decision plan.
e. The objectives are approved and validated by all stakeholders, and stakeholder access to health data has been defined and approved by the individual.
f. All health provision objectives are prioritized.
g. The HDMS will define how objectives are measured and evaluated.
h. The HDMS will define all communication and/or educational gaps, to include necessary or required training that effectively and efficiently supports identified patient care objectives.

2. Health Data Plan of Care

a. PHP: Health data integration
  i. Patient collects any/all healthcare records
b. PHP: Wellness management integration
  i. Patient establishes an active wellness program
  ii. Activate the wellness program
c. PHP: Finance management integration
  i. Patient will have/establish a health financial plan
  ii. Establish current coverage and or limitations
d. PHP: Personal health assessment integration
  i. Patient will actively monitor their ongoing health needs

3. Health Data Management Program

a. PHP has been established
  i. Patient demonstrates a mechanism to collect information
b. PHP has been organized
  i. Patient demonstrates an indexing process for information collected
c. PHP is in use by individual and assigned stakeholders
  i. Patient demonstrates tracking of consent and distribution/use of their personal health information
d. PHP updates, maintenance, and communications have been defined
  i. Patient demonstrates an interactive approach to ongoing updates of their personal health information

4. Health Data Governance

a. Data governance is structured
  i. Patient demonstrates a process to determine and validate access to their personal health information
b. Content to be governed is defined
  i. Patient demonstrates which information will be accessible and to whom
c. Policy and procedures are defined
  i. Patient collects relevant policy and procedures of the stakeholders involved with managing their care and information

   d. The program is active
      i. Patient will validate who is utilizing their personal health information, how, and to what degree (do they understand it)
   e. Technology is defined
      i. Patient will define the technology they will use in managing their health information and will understand the technology used by their providers

5. Health Data Architecture
   a. Identify the data
      i. As defined in Section III of this book
   b. Define the data
      i. As defined in Section III of this book
   c. Govern the data
      i. Patient will identify who will have access to their personal health information and will define limitations of access and dissemination (refer to content in Section III of this book)

6. Health Data Technology
   a. Technology architecture defined
      i. Defined and validated by the patient and advocate
   b. Data technology tool identified
      i. Defined and validated by the patient and advocate
   c. Data storage management strategy
      i. Defined and validated by the patient and advocate
   d. Risk planning established
      i. Defined and validated by the patient and advocate

7. Health Data Quality Program
   a. Data quality program established
      i. Defined and validated by the patient and advocate
   b. Quality of existing data established
      i. Defined and validated by the patient and advocate
   c. Quality of new data monitored
      i. Defined and validated by the patient and advocate

8. Health Data Control Environment
   a. Data control(s) identified and established
      i. Defined and validated by the patient and advocate
   b. Data controls and data management life cycle support established
      i. Defined and validated by the patient and advocate
   c. Patient health data integration within stakeholder team
      i. Defined and validated by the patient and advocate

Execution of the PHP Model (Defined Health Data Management Strategy)

This book highlights the role of the patient advocate as a valued resource for PHP model development and sustainment as a best practice. Patient advocates increase their overall performance effectiveness by enhancing their ability to understand basic human dynamics. In order to effectively help any individual, the advocate must develop a suitable patient-focused HDMS and clearly understand all defined objectives developed and agreed by the patient. If the patient is incapable or unable to clearly understand the issues or objectives at hand, then the advocate can facilitate the creation of health objectives with the individual and stakeholders. Section I provides a variety of perspectives on understanding people, communication styles, and work styles. Section II provides materials that help the individual to better understand the overall healthcare environment. Section III provides guidance on data collection points of health, wellness management, and financial and personal health assessments.

Patient Advocate Experience: A stakeholder such as an employer, payer, and/or provider invests heavily in systems, programs, and services; however, it often fails to yield savings on healthcare services and ultimately generates poor outcomes for the patient. **Lesson Learned:** If upfront investments are NOT made in assessing a patient's willingness and readiness to obtain and/or manage their own personal health data, the patient cannot maximize the benefit from provider data system investments, programs, and/or service offerings available to enable the best possible care.

PATIENT ADVOCACY INSTRUCTORS' REFERENCE GUIDES

I

> Education is the most powerful weapon you can use to change the world.
>
> **Nelson Mandela**
> *president of South Africa, political activist*

This section contains a series of reference guides to provide perspective on communicating with people. They are intended to add perspective. As advocates, our ability to communicate is just as important as having subject matter expertise. Information is useless if the recipient does not gain knowledge from it and therefore cannot act in their own best interest. Section I begins with a discussion on patient advocacy, with illustrative examples, and defines what is contained within a personal health record. This is followed by a commentary on the role of the patient advocate as a teacher.

As a patient advocate, the first step in the advocacy process is to assess and to listen to the patient. Listen to words, verbs, inflection, verbal, and nonverbal communication. Therefore, Section I of this book includes additional practice guides on information that will facilitate the understanding of people from a generational perspective, personality type, and feelings. This will provide cues about what to listen for. Once you get a sense of who the person is, the resources available, and what the person wants and needs, you can move toward helping. You cannot individualize your interventions until you understand the person first.

We are in the age of the customer. This concept is all about how consumers connect with the world of information around them. They are becoming increasingly empowered as their real-time access to information is just a click away. This age requires the ability to impact useable bits and bytes of information. The age of the customer is about personalized plans of care and the identification of specific customer needs. These practice guides are simply about understanding the human perspective and how humans interact with their environment and others.

Chapter 3

PHP Instructors' Guide to the Front Line

Patient Advocacy: Real-Life Drama

> The task of the modern educator is not to cut down jungles, but to irrigate deserts.

C.S Lewis
Novelist, poet, literary critic, essayist, Christian apologist

The following two stories reflect the experiences of a professional advocate acting on behalf of a patient and stress the importance of learning when to get help, asking the right questions, and developing a personal health record.

The first example reflects how a patient may be hurt by our healthcare system while navigating physician orders and insurance company complexities. The end result is a patient faced with long-term pain and ongoing suffering. The root cause? A market that is protocol driven, in which orders are executed with a strictly defined set of criteria. This is in comparison to a market that is data driven, in which orders are executed through specified sets of data points.

Our person of interest is a 45-year-old veteran intensive care nurse from Illinois. Her name is Sarah. In addition to her nursing career, she has worked for 15 years as a medical auditor of hospital bills and medical records. This is her experience:

> "I need help," she states. "I am in massive amounts of pain and cannot walk." She further elaborates that she had injured her knee that day by tripping and falling hard on a concrete curb, knee-first. She rated her pain as an 11 on a scale of 1 to 10, and when she went in to see her doctor, she was told that she may have torn a ligament in her right knee. "Should I get an MRI to understand the source of the pain?" she asked, "No," the doctor responded. Upon physical examination, she

was told: "You have to go to physical therapy for six weeks." She asked, "What exactly is wrong with my knee? I have never been in this much pain before." He followed up with "I am not sure; however, your insurance company will not pay for an MRI unless you go to physical therapy for six weeks first."

Barely able to walk, she attended her first physical therapy session, but her distress only continued from there. The therapist had no idea why she was experiencing such a high level of discomfort. Regardless, the therapist continued the session without an understanding as to why her pain was increasing throughout.

As Sarah left the session, she collapsed from the pain on her way out the door and sprained her ankle. Now she had two injuries to deal with. In the evening, she contacted her patient advocate. "I am in so much pain I don't know what to do!" Her advocate advised her, "You have no choice. Go to the ER—now."

The emergency room staff did a physical exam and a "Doppler study" (avoiding the MRI scan that would have cost about $2220), and determined that Sarah had in fact injured a ligament. She had also developed a cyst (a pocket of blood below the knee from the original injury) and the therapist had ruptured the cyst during the physical therapy session. The blood had nowhere to go except under her knee cap. The blood sitting within the knee cap was the cause of the unbearable pain and subsequent visit to the emergency room with a price tag in excess of $7000. The insurance company's refusal to cover the $2220 cost of an MRI thus resulted in an *additional* expenditure of $5000. This continuance of long-term costly complications and unnecessary suffering was because the injury was not properly assessed and treated. And the $7000 total bill didn't include extra costs associated with the sprained ankle—a direct result of the insurance company's requirement for physical therapy. Five years later, Sarah is continuing to receive treatment for this injury.

Keep in mind that Sarah was an experienced, registered nurse and medical auditor. Despite her expertise and experience as a healthcare professional, she *still* fell through the cracks of the healthcare system. Imagine what the typical consumer has to endure. This could be YOU!

Lesson Learned: The conversation between a doctor and a patient (whether he or she is a nurse *or not*) should never be, "This is the care I recommend based on what will be paid." Still, this disturbing story repeats itself daily among many people. This situation not only causes higher insurance costs but also compromises the doctor due to rules imposed by third parties.

What else can go wrong?

Let's take a look at our friend, Doug, as another example. Doug's story represents what it is like to be stranded within the healthcare and employee benefits system. He is an accomplished investment banker who lives in New York and has been battling with multiple myeloma.

He has and continues to have ongoing health and disability insurance coverage. They range from the employee benefits department's failure to inform him of his options, to actually obtaining the benefits services he is entitled to by his employee benefits package. How did he get stuck?

The Route to Confusion: His employer neglected to inform Doug of his rights to obtain disability benefits while he was employed. His company's benefits department instead offered Doug a few paid weeks off to deal with his illness. Eventually, his division of the company was shut down and he was out of a job. Though he had actually requested an application for disability benefits from human resources, they never provided him with the form while he was an employee even though the company was aware of his condition. Once he was laid off, he lost his rights to obtain benefits under the company's disability policy. What happened next was only the beginning of his healthcare nightmare.

> Engulfed in stress, Doug called his patient advocate and explained, "XXX insurance company is denying my doctor's recommendation for a stem cell transplant. They are telling me it is experimental and will not pay for it at this time."
> His patient advocate already had a file of Doug's prior medical bills. He was aware of Doug's insurance company from prior audit experience and knew that this kind of service had been paid for before by the carrier. The advocate assisted Doug in writing a letter to his insurance company that said: "Please tell me what ICD-9CM code and respective CPT codes were utilized to render an opinion that my doctor's recommendation was experimental?" As instructed by his advocate, Doug faxed and mailed the letter to the claims supervisor. Lo and behold, 7 days later, Doug contacted his advocate and was very excited as he had just received a letter stating that they would cover the procedure.

Lesson Learned: If you do not understand the world of International Classification of Diseases (ICD) and current procedural terminology (CPT) codes, you are like most Americans with healthcare insurance, unaware of how these codes work together and carry specific meaning. For example, at a minimum, every patient should know that ICD codes are diagnostic codes that communicate *why* something is being done to a patient, while CPT codes communicate *what* is being done to the patient. Therefore, each healthcare transaction should communicate what is being done and why. Healthcare coding systems are highly technical elements and contribute to the convoluted healthcare system. The problem is that, without this understanding, *you cannot fully advocate for yourself.* But before you start cursing your doctor when you run into a problem like Doug's, remember that there are legitimate doctors who are as frustrated as you when their plan of care is driven by complicated third party organizations rules that do not allow for individual consideration.

The bottom line is that as healthcare continues to evolve and become even more complicated than it already is, it becomes increasingly important for each person to learn how to advocate for themselves. Enlisting an experienced advocate can be a great benefit while navigating the daunting complexity of the healthcare system.

Without a patient advocate, Sarah would not have received the assistance she needed while experiencing such severe pain. Patients in pain are often compromised in their ability to effectively advocate for themselves. Her personal health portfolio (PHP) helped her efforts in negotiating with ongoing providers regarding the clinical root cause of her suffering. And through patient advocacy support, Doug eventually received his disability benefits along with approval for a lifesaving procedure.

PHP: What It Is

A PHP—also referred to as a personal healthcare record (PHR)—is a detailed personal health and financial record that patients use to assist themselves in navigating the ambiguous maze of healthcare. It allows them to get the care they need and are entitled to, without getting lost in the system and without unnecessary delay.

The PHP will be discussed throughout this book. In addition, the appendix provides an introductory version of the information each patient should have at all times. You can also find the same guidance at www.mbaaudit.com under the Health$hield Program. Doug utilized his portfolio to navigate through the healthcare system and advocate for himself with minimal support, and Sarah continued to use an advocate, simply as a resource for collaboration.

Patient Message: Learn when you need to get help, develop a personal healthcare portfolio record, and learn how to ask the right questions.

Chapter 4

PHP Instructors' Guide on Patient Advocate as Teacher

Wisdom begins with wonder.

Socrates
Greek philosopher

The goal of patient advocacy is to become a guide, navigator, and ultimately a teacher. What makes an individual a good teacher? Let's break it down into two components. The first is a proficient understanding of the subject matter. Knowledge of the healthcare market and, at a minimum, where to go to get answers to questions are essential. The second part is the delivery of that knowledge to another person. Some individuals may be great technical experts in their field; however, their ability to impart knowledge may need some work.

When asked what makes a good teacher,* a group of high school students listed some of the following aspects:

- Treat students with respect
- Be enthusiastic
- Know your stuff
- Be available for extra help
- Use multimedia resources
- Connect with students/form relationships
- Don't lecture for the whole class—mix things up
- Use web resources: Class site or blog, and review materials that students can access at home
- Be flexible

* www.techlearning.com list of what makes a good teacher—created by students.

Now compare some of those items with the *nine characteristics of a great teacher** described by Dr. Maria Orlando, who has evaluated hundreds of teachers:

- A great teacher respects students.
- A great teacher creates a sense of community and belonging in the classroom.
- A great teacher is warm, accessible, enthusiastic and caring.
- A great teacher sets high expectations for all students.
- A great teacher has his or her own love of learning.
- A great teacher is a skilled leader.
- A great teacher can "shift gears."
- A great teacher collaborates with colleagues on an ongoing basis.
- A great teacher maintains professionalism in all areas.

Now substitute *patient advocate* for the word *teacher*, and *patients* for *students*. The resemblance is striking.

Respectful

The number one aspect on both lists is respect. Caregiving comes with the responsibility of being compassionate and understanding. The patient advocate connects with their patients to form relationships. They know how to create an atmosphere of confidence and trust, letting the patient and his or her family feel a sense of community. Your patient advocate should demonstrate that your ideas and opinions are valued. Your patient advocate should have excellent communication skills with an ability to deliver content of all types in a calm, healing way. Coupled with the ability to simplify complicated medical terminology, an advocate becomes a useful resource.

Enthusiastic, Accessible

Next on both lists was enthusiasm, accessibility, and flexibility. A patient advocate must be dedicated to their job and arrive every day with a sense of trust and respect. Patients need to feel that their advocate is eager to help them communicate with a doctor, recommend a lab or medication, and emotionally support them through their frustration with the healthcare system. Patient advocates are good listeners, leaving their own personal problems out of the conversation. A patient needs to know their advocate is accessible to them and will maintain a caring attitude when called upon in an emergency. The patient advocate needs

---

* www.facultyfocus.com/articles/philosophy-of-teaching/nine-characteristics-of-a-great-teacher

to be flexible and understanding, knowing that on numerous occasions schedules need to be changed and hands need to be held.

Subject Matter Expert

Patient advocates must stay up to date with their knowledge. The best patient advocates never stop learning. If there is something they don't know, they will research the answer. They will likely understand the pros and cons of recommended treatments/procedures and will be able to relay that information to the patient. They also know that relaying too much information at once can be overwhelming, so they will package information based on priority and relay it in increments that would be more easily understood. An advocate's passion for learning will encourage their patient to take a greater interest in their own well-being.

Collaborator

The patient advocate can be the bridge that connects the patient and their doctor, much like a teacher collaborates with other teachers to form the best curriculum for their students. Many times, the advocate acts as a type of surrogate doctor, helping a patient understand what was just said in the exam room and explaining the side effects of medications. Due to the high demands on a physician's time for maintaining accurate medical health records and complying with ever-changing rules and regulations, they are sometimes too busy to sit and explain all of their findings and recommendations. Your advocate can meet with the physician to understand their care directives. The advocate will be very conscious of the fact that an irritable nurse may not be able to listen properly and thereby miss a crucial detail. They can pick up cues from other caregivers and teach you how to spot them for yourself.

Resource

A patient advocate maintains access to a multitude of resources. Multimedia resources, apps, and all types of web resources are available just by asking. The advocate can help maneuver through the patient provider's web site to make an appointment, send an e-mail, or get a result. They can also help to look for a specialist qualified in the care needed by the health plan. They can help you download apps to manage your medical records (such as the forms in the appendix of this book) or answer questions about medical definitions of diseases or medications, for example. A patient advocate will be the first to caution on not believing everything one reads on the Internet, as advances in treatments happen every day.

Cheerleader

A patient advocate will set the proper priorities for medical care and treatment. "Nothing but the best" is their mantra when it comes to a patient's health. As they invest their time in getting to know the patient, an advocate will formulate a plan to navigate the system to ensure that the patient is directed to the most competent providers. They will encourage and support the patient as they undergo treatment and new regimens of care.

Patient Advocate Experience: As a patient advocate, learn to understand your own strengths, weaknesses, and limitations. Conduct self-assessments and illicit feedback on the impact you are having with your patient.

Lessons Learned: Advocates are faced with their own vulnerabilities and limitations. Do not take on a case in which you feel that you cannot be effective. The next practice guide will review the impact of generational perspectives in the role of the patient advocate.

Chapter 5

PHP Instructors' Guide on People and a Generational Perspective

Knowledge in a vacuum is meaningless.

Endsley, Bolte, Jones
Authors, Designing Situational Awareness

Patient advocates serve individuals with a range of generational profiles. Patient advocacy will take on different meanings based on an individual's age, condition, and tasks required. Patient advocates or patient navigators provide general assistance to patients and caregivers as they maneuver their way through the healthcare system. Individuals may find themselves advocating on their own behalf or on behalf of a family or multiple individuals.

The explosion of healthcare data and the rush to protect it mandates ALL of us to be mindful of the medical information we have amassed throughout the years and to be able to defend it against any assault. Effective educators/advocates should adapt their approaches based on the characteristics and ability of the individual patient/family unit. This guide is intended to provide a brief generational perspective profile. The understanding and considerations may promote effective communication approaches. Ultimately, any patient advocate will have to rely on their training, education, and experience to define the most effective advocate approach.

The following is a description of each current generational profile. Included are famous individual quotes on a particular life perspective. Each generation includes a quote taken from a current day individual on their perspective and expectations of healthcare providers.

Understanding the Mindset of Generational Perspectives[*][†][‡]

Twentieth Century[§]

The Greatest Generation

- **G.I. Generation, 1901–1924:** This generation experienced in full magnitude the effects of World War II, both in battle and at home. Personality traits included being assertive, energetic doers; they were often noted to be excellent team players, were community-minded and strongly interested in personal morality, and had near-absolute standards of right and wrong. They had a strong sense of personal civic duty, which means that they voted. Marriage was for life, divorce and having children out of wedlock were not accepted, and strong loyalty was shown to jobs, groups, and schools. There was no retirement—you worked until you died or couldn't work anymore. They were a labor-union-spawning generation. "Use it up, fix it up, and make it do, or do without." Avoid debt, save up, and buy with cash.[¶]

Greatest Generation Patient Advocate Perspective:

When working with patients in this category, it is imperative to respect their autonomy. They've lived long, have been through a lot, have strong opinions, and may be stubborn about care options.

Greatest Generation Current Day Patient Interview Response:

I listen to my doctor, who does not have time to listen, and then I do what I want to do.

Ninety-nine-year-old woman

Supporting Quotes from the G.I. Generation:

We are taught you must blame your father, your sisters, your brothers, the school, and teachers—but never blame yourself. It's never your fault. But it's always your fault, because if you wanted to change you're the one who has got to change.

Katharine Hepburn[**]
actress, born 1907

---

[*] Straus, William, Howe, Neil, "Generations: The History of America's Future, 1584 to 2069."

[†] http://www.esds1.pt/site/images/stories/isacosta/secondary_pages/10%C2%BA_block1/Generations%20Chart.pdf

[‡] http://poptop.hypermart.net/generation.html

[§] http://www.esds1.pt/site/images/stories/isacosta/secondary_pages/10%C2%BA_block1/Generations%20Chart.pdf

[¶] http://www.marketingteacher.com/the-six-living-generations-in-america/

[**] http://www.great-quotes.com/quotes/author/Katharine/Hepburn/pg/3

I do not like broccoli. And I haven't liked it since I was a little kid and my mother made me eat it. And I'm President of the United States and I'm not going to eat any more broccoli.

George H. Bush
former U.S. president, born 1924

■ **Silent Generation, 1925–1945:** The label refers to their conformist and civic instincts. This generation was born between two World Wars. Too young to participate, they often had fathers who went off to fight. Attributes of this group include pre-feminism: women generally stayed home to raise children, and if they worked it was only at certain jobs such as teaching, nursing, or secretarial work. Men pledged loyalty to their corporation, meaning that once you got a job, you generally kept it for life. These are the richest, most free-spending retirees in history. Like the G.I. Generation, marriage was for life, and divorce and having children out of wedlock were not acceptable. In grade school, the gravest teacher complaints were about passing notes and chewing gum in class. They are avid readers, especially of newspapers. Retirement to them means to sit in a rocking chair and live your final days in peace. They were the big band/swing music generation, and have a strong sense of transgenerational common values with near-absolute truths. Disciplined, self-sacrificing, and cautious, they were the first hopeful drumbeats for civil rights.

Silent Generation Patient Advocate Perspective:

This generation is not accustomed to the current modes of communication; they are used to a hands-on environment. Frustration with recent healthcare mandates will often result in the patient feeling lost and short-changed.

Silent Generation Current Day Patient Interview:

"The doctors don't care anymore. They put your file down, do not remember the advice they gave you, nor give you the information you need to know. I don't trust them." This was a 73-year-old female patient who developed a parathyroid tumor and was not informed about it until one year later.

Supporting Quotes from the Silent Generation:

Of all the forms of inequality, injustice in healthcare is the most shocking and inhumane.

Martin Luther King
activist, born 1929, in a speech to the
Medical Committee for Human Rights, 1966

You take your problems to a God, but what you really need is for the God to take you to the inside of you.

Tina Turner
singer/songwriter, born 1939

Baby Boomers

■ **Boom Generation/Hippies, 1946–1964:** This generation was born during the fertility spike after World War II, which ended with the introduction of the birth control pill. It falls into two subsets, the "save-the-world revolutionaries" of the 1960s and 1970s and the "party-hardy career climbers (Yuppies)" of the 1970s/1980s. This generation includes the "me" generation as well as the rock and roll music generation. It ushered in "free love" and societal non-violent protests, which triggered violence. Self-righteous and self-centeredness with a "buy it now" and "use credit" attitude were attributes. Individuals were too busy for much neighborly involvement, yet had strong desires to reset or change the common values for the good of all. Even though their mothers were generally housewives, responsible for all child-rearing, women of this generation began working outside the home in record numbers, thereby changing the entire nation as this was the first generation to have children raised in a two-income household where the mother was not omnipresent. This was also the first TV generation, as well as the first divorce generation, as divorce began to be accepted as a tolerable reality. Optimistic, driven, and team-oriented, this generation tends to be more positive about authority, hierarchal structure, and tradition and is one of the largest generations in history, with 77 million people.

Baby Boomer Patient Advocate Perspective:

This generation will most likely be faced with managing their own medical issues as well as those of their kids and aging parents.

Baby Boomer Current Day Patient Interview Response:

If I needed healthcare, I'd go to the Internet and look up U.S. News & World Report for "best doctors." From there I'd seek out the specialty and proceed to investigate proximity and whether they accept my insurance. The healthcare system is a nightmare—not that that's any news, but it is worse today. I have noticed that doctors are declining more and more patients **because of their insurance (*as opposed to the lack of insurance*)**. My mother's GP doesn't want to take on patients who seem "irresponsible" toward their medicine because Medicare will withhold payment if the patient's condition remains the same or worsens (e.g., blood sugar levels remain high in diabetics). My dermatologist, one of the most respected professionals in his field, is no longer accepting patients' insurance (they pay cash and are reimbursed by the insurance company) for simple checkups and follow ups.

Fifty-four-year-old male patient and caregiver to a family member

Supporting Quotes from Baby Boomers:

The roles we play in each other's lives are only as powerful as the trust and connection between us—the protection, safety, and caring we are willing to share.

Oprah Winfrey
actress and talk show host, born 1954

My body could handle the crutches but my mind couldn't stand the sideline.

Michael Jordan
pro athlete, born 1963

Generation X

■ **Baby Busters, 1965–1980:** This is the post-peak boomer era in which the number of children born per household dropped. Women were choosing not to have children, and the notion of women simply saying no to procreation was an option and an acceptable choice.

Generation X Patient Advocate Perspective:

Independence, a need for efficiency, and confidence in the system are primary focuses for these Baby Busters.

Generation X Current Day Patient Interview Response:

The "go to" for us is me. I read our policy twice before we signed up. It is really hard to navigate the current healthcare system. It takes so much time and services are always delayed.

A second interview response:

What healthcare system? We don't have healthcare in place in this country. Presently, and for the past several decades, America has illness care, disease care, and many other types of care making sure people's health gets corrupted and rarely gets better. If I need help with my health I would only visit one person, and that's myself. I don't trust anyone else.

Forty-five-year-old independent, unmarried female without children and in a committed relationship

Supporting Quotes from Baby Busters:

Humans have a knack for choosing precisely the things that are worst for them.*

J.K. Rowling
author, born 1965

I am pretty health-conscious, so when my girlfriend and/or I make dinner—no, I don't have a cook—we choose the healthier options: lean meats, steamed veggies, fish, etc. Of course, there are always those cravings for the "bad foods" that I do give in to once in a while.†

Tiger Woods
golf pro, born 1975

■ **MTV Generation/Boomerang Generation, 1975–1985:** Young adults in the Western world are focused on and influenced by fashion trends and music in this generation. They have also been referred to as the "Doom Generation," due to the popularity of the 1993 computer game *Doom*. As adults, this generation tends to be affluent, stable, and saddled with responsibility as their parents were at the same age.‡ Attributes include entrepreneurial and very individualistic tendencies. Government and big business mean little to them. They want to save the neighborhood, not the world, and feel misunderstood by other generations. Cynical of many major institutions, which failed them or their parents during their formative years, they are therefore eager to make marriage work and be there for their children. They don't feel like a generation, but they are. Raised in the transition phase of written-based knowledge to digital knowledge archives, most remember being in school without computers and afterwards the introduction of computers in middle school or high school. They desire a chance to learn, explore, and make a contribution, as well as having a tendency to commit to self rather than to an organization or specific career. This generation averages seven career changes in their lifetime, with working for a company for life no longer seen as the norm, unlike previous generations. Society, and thus individuals, is seen as disposable. AIDS began to spread during this generation and was the first lethal infectious disease in the history of any culture on earth which was not subjected to any quarantine. School problems were about drugs. This generation is late to marry after cohabitation, quick to divorce, and includes many single parents. Self-image tended

---

* http://www.brainyquote.com/quotes/authors/j/j_k_rowling.html#U4c0E0vK88rh2Tro.99
† http://quotes.yourdictionary.com/author/tiger-woods/120709#KZXMtRAhp7wiMU4f.99
‡ https://www.metlife.com/assets/cao/mmi/publications/mmi-pressroom/2013/mmi-gen-x-pr.pdf

to revolve around labels and brand names. They want what they want and want it now, but with a lack of monetary power, most are in deep in credit card debt.

MTV Patient Advocate Perspective:

This group has been exposed to technology and may have the affluence to afford services, but may also easily find themselves overextended and are mainly reliant on social media for information.

MTV Current Day Patient Interview Response #1:

I would call the Obamacare toll-free number and take it from there. I also would use the Internet to find answers to any questions I might have.

Thirty-two-year-old male, working full-time

MTV Current Day Patient Interview Response #2:

I would ask a doctor friend. Then start the process. The VA is a joke. I asked for an annual physical on January 4th and was scheduled for March 28th. My United Healthcare premiums have gone up 400% since Obamacare. It's best to go to Mexico for healthcare.

Thirty-year-old male sales professional

MTV Current Day Patient Interview Response #3:

The healthcare system is set up for healthy people and is not for those who have chronic conditions. It seems like providers actually get annoyed when you come in to get help. Worse yet, they seem to only have general knowledge and not deep knowledge of any particular condition. In fact, it goes beyond the risk of medical errors, as these conditions can result in your death.

Thirty-four-year-old male with hemophilia

Supporting Quotes from the MTV/Boomerang Generation:

Of course, I want to be number one. But being happy and healthy is the most important thing.*

Venus Williams
tennis pro, born 1980

---

* http://www.inspirationalstories.com/quotes/t/venus-williams-on-health/

The question I ask myself almost every day is: 'Am I doing the most important thing I could be doing?' ... Unless I feel like I'm working on the most important problem that I can help with, then I'm not going to feel good about how I'm spending my time.

Mark Zuckerberg
entrepreneur, born 1984

Generation Y

■ **Echo Boom or 9/11 Generation, 1981–2000:** This generation is known for choosing to cohabitate with their parents after a brief launch from the home front. They are part of the boomerang generation. This generation was significantly exposed to the rise of mass communication, social media, and the Internet. They are nurtured by omnipresent parents and are optimistic and focused. Respect authority, falling crime rates, and falling teen pregnancy rates are attributes. But with school safety problems, they have to live with the thought that they could be shot at school; they learned early that the world is not a safe place. They schedule everything and experience enormous academic pressure. They feel like a generation, have great expectations for themselves, and prefer digital literacy as they grew up in a digital environment. They get all their information and most of their socialization from the Internet. They prefer to work in teams, and with unlimited access to information, they tend to be assertive with strong views. They envision the world as a 24/7 place and want fast and immediate processing. They are accustomed to receiving positive feedback. They do not live to work, but they prefer a more relaxed work environment with a lot of closely guided assistance and accolades.

Generation Y Patient Advocate Perspective:

This group is often health conscious but not actively managing a personal health record. Most are likely to still be reliant on an adult parent if in the boomerang category. Patient engagement will most likely require the use of technology.

Generation Y Current Day Patient Interview Response #1:

Don't talk to me if it is not on a mobile device.
Twenty-two-year-old male college student

Generation Y Current Day Patient Interview Response #2

Thinking about my healthcare information and records, I realized that my parents take care of everything. All I have to do is make a call to set up the appointment and go to the doctor; everything after that, my parents take care of. I don't know the first thing when it comes to orga-nizing my records or how the insurance works.

Twenty-one-year-old female, working part-time while attending college

Supporting Quotes from the Echo Boom or 9/11 Generation:

I am 26 and, and I don't recover as fast as I have in the past.*

Michael Phelps
athlete, born 1985

Rules for healthy living: "diet, exercise, and writing help her stay happy and balanced."†

Taylor Swift
singer/songwriter, born 1989

Twenty-First Century

■ **Generation Z:** The "Boomlets" or "New Silent Generation" experts differ on when the earliest members of Generation Z (from 1990 to born after 2001) were born‡. This group is often referred to as "Generation V" for virtual, or "Generation C" for community or content. The new silent generation is a Google generation. They are being raised with a cell phone, and grew up with video games and DVD players. Rather than being eco-friendly, they have eco-fatigue: a tiredness of hearing about the environment and the many reasons we have to save it. With the advent of computers and web-based learning, children leave toys behind at a younger and younger age and are called "KGOY kids" (kids growing older younger). Many companies have suffered because of this, most recognizably Mattel, the maker of Barbie dolls. In the 1990s, the average age of a child in their target market was 10 years old, but in 2000 it dropped to 3 years old. As children reach the ages of four and five, old enough to play on the computer, they become less interested in toys and begin to desire electron-ics such as cell phones and video games. They are savvy consumers and know what they want and how to get it, and are oversaturated with brands.

Generation Z Patient Advocate Perspective:

Within this age group, healthcare and managing health will most likely not be on the radar unless the individual has an active health condition.

---

* http://www.brainyquote.com/quotes/authors/m/michael_phelps.html#sH7ipmjbPTQOTdYp.99
† http://www.webmd.com/women/features/taylor-swifts-rules-for-healthy-living?page=2
‡ https://en.wikipedia.org/wiki/Generation_Z

Patient engagement will assume the use of technology. Individuals will not be tolerant of provider infrastructures that are not patient centric. Expect providers who do not understand the patient as a consumer to no longer exist with this generation.

Generation Z Patient Interview Response:

As long as I can keep track of everything with my watch. I think all doctor appointments, reminders, and test results are going to be done by a watch, like the one in the movie *Spy Kids*. It's called a Hologram 3D watch. You tap it and a projection pops up. It will show the results for you to see and then you will be able to file them in the watch to show a doctor when you visit. All appointments and reminders will be done with the watch.

Fifteen-year-old female high school freshman

Supporting Quotes from Generation Z

No matter what problems we are facing, there's always room for happiness in our lives.*

Sam Berns
progeria patient, born 1996

I dance every day of the week after school and go to competitions on the weekends.†

Brooke Hyland
dancer, born 1998

Patient Advocate Experience: Imagine the following scenario. A healthcare professional (who is a millennial) working with a family that includes a patient who is part of the Greatest Generation, two baby boomer children with healthcare issues themselves, and an MTV generation sibling.

Lesson Learned: If the millennial healthcare provider is unable to adapt their message, critical information will not be exchanged among the parties. The result can range from unmet expectations to poor patient outcomes. The next practice guide will facilitate recognizing personality types and considerations for working with these individuals, in addition to the education perspective.

---

* http://lifeaccordingtosam.com/#/about-sam/
† http://brooke-hyland-official.weebly.com/interviews.html

Chapter 6

PHP Instructors' Guide on Myers-Briggs Personality Types

Anyone who stops learning is old, whether at twenty or eighty. Anyone who keeps learning stays young.

Henry Ford
founder of Ford Motor Company

The Briggs Myers personality types* provide another perspective to understanding people. Consider this reference tool as a supplement to the generational perspective. It is not intended for the advocate to perform or apply this test. Remember, the patient advocate role is a person-to-person role versus a person-to-plasticrole. The purpose of this supplement is to provide perspective on how different personality types may function at work, home, or in a relationship, as well as how they will respond to the advocate, their follow-up, and eventual self-advocacy.

The following is a sample summary illustration of personality-type profiles:[†]

IDENTIFIERS:	**E = Extroverted**	**N = Intuitive**
	F = Feeling	**P = Perceiving**
	I = Introverted	**S = Sensing**
	J = Judging	**T = Thinking**

- **The Healer** (Introverted, Intuitive, Feeling, and Perceiving—**INFP**). Poetic, kind, altruistic, and eager to help a good cause—Healers are imaginative idealists, guided by their own core values and beliefs. To a Healer, possibilities are paramount; the realism of the moment is only a passing concern. They may initially seem cool, as they reserve their most authentic thoughts and feelings

---

* http://www.truity.com/view/types, accessed 1/4/2016
† http://www.truity.com/personality-type/INFP, accessed 1/6/2016

for people they know well. They are reflective, spiritual, and often interested in having meaningful conversations about values, ethics, people, and personal growth. Being great listeners, sensitive to others, open-minded, nonjudgmental, and able to make decisions based on gut feelings make them great mediators, counselors, and educators. This personality trait comprises 4% of the population. **Patient advocate perspective:** This individual may be more gut-driven and is at risk of ignoring concrete data. The tendency to be in denial mode may result in not keeping active health issues on the conscious radar.

- **The Counselor** (Introverted, Intuitive, Feeling, and Judging—*INFJ*). Quiet, mystical, inspiring idealists, Counselors are energized by taking personal moments of solidarity. They see patterns and possibilities, prioritize people and emotions, and prefer structure and order. INFJ types are idealistic, creative, introspective, authentic, and reserved. With the ability to be intuitive of others' emotions and motivations, they will often know how someone else is feeling before that person knows it themselves. They can usually be found pursuing humanitarian careers in healthcare, counseling, education, and religion. They are the least common personality type in the population, comprising only 2% of adults. **Patient advocate perspective:** The risk faced by these individuals is their tendency to be focused on helping other versus themselves. They may need coaching on becoming effective communicators of their own health issues during interactions with their provider.

- **The Teacher** (Extroverted, Intuitive, Feeling, and Judging—*ENFJ*). Charismatic, inspiring, and mesmerizing, the Teacher personality type is known for their friendly, "can't we all just get along" humanitarian effect. That, coupled with the gift for seeing potential in others and being skilled motivators, makes them excellent teachers and readers. Dynamic, productive, and organized, with a belief in total cooperation, also makes them good event planners and educational guides. However, they typically have too much on their plates and can overextend themselves. This trait comprises 3% of the population. **Patient advocate perspective:** The patient advocate may need to coach this individual to ensure that they obtain details of their health information from providers, spend time reviewing the information, and then utilize the information to make detailed informed decisions. This may require coaching on setting priorities with their own healthcare as well as the healthcare of other family/friends they are helping.

- **The Champion** (Extroverted, Intuitive, Feeling, and Perceiving—*ENFP*). Enthusiastic, creative, and socially a free spirit, the Champion is always ready with a smile. The Champion, or Campaigner, is typically an agile and expressive communicator, using wit and humor to create engaging stories. People are a priority, and Champions love to ponder what makes people tick and are energized through spending time with others. They can be artistic and unconventional, preferring imagination than details. Champions comprise a large portion (8%) of the population. **Patient advocate perspective:** These patients may need help dealing with healthcare facts and collecting the information necessary to build their personal healthcare portfolio.

■ *The Mastermind* (Introverted, Intuitive, Thinking, and Judging—*INTJ*). Also known as the Architect, the Mastermind is an imaginative, strategic thinker, with a plan for everything. Masterminds are analytical problem solvers, eager to improve systems and processes with their innovative ideas. They can be lifelong learners, bent on self-improvement. Because their decisions are based on logic and analytics, they gravitate to careers in science, research, technology, data management, business, or law. They can be reserved, serious, and selective about their relationships. The Mastermind personality trait comprises about 2% of the population. **Patient advocate perspective:** This person may need help selecting a provider who will be just as serious about their healthcare as they are. If he or she does have a long-term health plan, your review and advice would be welcome.

■ *The Commander* (Extroverted, Intuitive, Thinking, and Judging—*ENTJ*). Bold, imaginative, and strong-willed leaders, the Commander will find a way or make a new one. Commanders are ambitious, strategic, career-oriented leaders, organizing people and processes to achieve their goals. They can be decisive, blunt, and direct, and don't believe in wasting time taking into account other people's sensitivity. Commanders are reactive to issues of power and tend to take on jobs as top executives in science, engineering, or healthcare, or as strategists, judges, or officers in the military. Personally, they expect a lot from others and some may say that working is what they do for fun. Commanders comprise 2% of the population and are mostly male. **Patient advocate perspective:** Patience may be required to educate this patient on the pitfalls and roadblocks in healthcare. They may be too busy to capture all the details necessary for a complete healthcare portfolio.

■ *The Visionary* (Extroverted, Innovative, Thinking, and Perceiving—*ENTP*). The Visionary, sometimes known as the Debater, is clever, analytical, imaginative, and characteristically entrepreneurial. Open-minded and unconventional, Visionaries want to analyze, understand, and influence other people. They can be nontraditional explorers, always keeping their options open. They are masters of reinventing the wheel and often refuse to do a task the same way twice. Visionaries are happy to "live and let live," but can get bored with people that can't keep up with them. They typically gravitate to management and leadership roles in science, engineering, finance, or education. Visionaries make up 3% of the population. **Patient advocate perspective:** This patient may not like living by the new managed care rules and you may have to convince them of the importance of following them.

■ *The Architect* (Introverted, Innovative, Thinking, and Perceiving—*INTP*). Also known as the Logician, Architects are innovative inventors with an unquenchable thirst for knowledge. Sometimes called "free-spirited idea mills and absentminded professors," they can be a plethora of creativity. They are philosophical, seeking to understand the mysteries of the universe. They can be intense, blunt, and favor autonomy. Experts say that they are perhaps the most intellectually profound of all the types. Architects tend to be engineers, scientists, doctors, lawyers, technical writers, or software developers. They comprise 3% of the population. **Patient advocate perspective:** This patient will not want to be bothered with the drudgery of tracking medical concerns. Easy-to-complete forms might be best for them.

■ *The Provider* (Extroverted, Sensing, Feeling, and Judging—*ESFJ*). The Provider is an extraordinarily caring, conscientious, and social person. Always eager to help, their sense of responsibility for other people's needs makes them excellent caretakers and successful at working with children. Organized and attentive to detail, they always want to make order out of chaos. They are punctual, have a strict moral code, and are hard workers. They want things to be right with people around them and may be outspoken and urge others to "stick to the script." Roles such as committee leaders, event planners, and church volunteers suit them well. Their careers generally range from education, counseling, and healthcare to any position requiring attention to detail (medical, mechanical, technician, assistant, etc.). This is the second most popular personality trait in the United States, comprising 12% of the population. **Patient advocate perspective:** Providers may find themselves selecting a practitioner/facility based on facts rather than feelings, and need help with worrying about themselves instead of others.

■ *The Performer* (Extroverted, Sensing, Feeling, and Perceiving—*ESFP*). An entertainer at heart, the Performer is impulsive, energetic, and enthusiastic. Life is never boring around them. Performers are talkative, fun-loving, and like to be in the middle of the action and the center of attention. They are spontaneous, sometimes to the point of overextending their calendars. Performers love to entertain, bringing people together via games, sports, cooking, and other events. However, they are grounded in reality and are usually keenly aware of the facts and details in their life. Performers prefer action careers in education, healthcare, and service organizations as well as physical action careers such as law enforcement, firefighting, or physical fitness. Performers comprise 9% of the population, with more women than men. **Patient advocate perspective:** Performers may be naturally responsive to participating in wellness-type programs. Tool offerings that may be helpful are those that facilitate time management and organization.

■ *The Protector* (Introverted, Sensing, Feeling, and Judging—*ISFJ*). Also known as the Defender, the Protector is always ready to safeguard their loved ones. The protectors are loyal, responsible traditionalists and enjoy contributing to society. Protectors are hardworking, compassionate listeners and prefer stable family relationships, thus many act as family historians and caregivers as well as volunteers. The Protector will take a job in healthcare, education, or caregiving. Their hands-on proclivity and attention to detail will also place them in the business world as secretaries or assistants. Protectors comprise the most common trait at 14%. **Patient advocate perspective:** Caregiving personalities already, these patients understand the need to have a complete medical record and assist all of their loved ones in creating one too. This can reduce the extent of the advocate's role to simply providing helpful advice.

■ *The Composer* (Introverted, Sensing, Feeling, and Perceiving—*ISFP*). The Composer, also known as the Adventurer, is flexible, charming, and always ready to explore and experience something new. The Composer lives in the moment, finds beauty in their surroundings, and has a strong sense of the aesthetic. They have finely tuned artistic sensibilities and are easily reactive to color, texture, and tone. They "go with the flow," preferring to stay in the background and let their actions speak for them. Being both observant and helpful, Composers can be found in law enforcement, firefighting, pharmacy, nursing, social work, fitness, and cosmetology. Composers comprise 9% of the population. **Patient advocate perspective:** This personality type may need help with sitting still long enough to take the time to complete the mundane tasks of documenting and recording their medical info.

■ *The Supervisor* (Extroverted, Sensing, Thinking, and Judging—*ESTJ*). The Supervisor, or Executive, is unsurpassed at managing things or people and is more likely to exhibit Type A behavior. The Supervisor likes to get things done, and done right. While sometimes demanding their way or the highway, they hold themselves to the highest degree of standards. Supervisors like to get things done in a systematic, logical way and take the initiative to establish processes and guidelines to keep order. Bank officers, financial managers, business owners, doctors, engineers, and consultants typically have the Supervisor trait. In addition, as they like to develop tangible products, you may see them in agriculture, production, or technology careers. Supervisors also comprise 9% of the population. **Patient advocate perspective:** This Type A personality may just need you to look over his or her work to see if anything was missed. He or she would be grateful for suggestions on perfecting his or her healthcare portfolio.

■ *The Dynamo* (Extroverted, Sensing, Thinking, and Perceiving—*ESTP*). The Dynamo, or Entrepreneur, is smart, energetic, and perceptive. They flirt with danger and like living on the edge. They are highly coordinated and often natural athletes. They are flirtatious, chatty, and highly energetic— often the life of the party. They select careers in business (sales and management); hands-on industries such as engineering, mechanics, or construction; and careers with risk, such as the military, law enforcement, or emergency medicine. The Dynamo makes up 4% of the population. **Patient advocate perspective:** This personality may disregard the use of excessive details in favor of a comprehensive portfolio. If they are in high-risk categories, they may need your advice on ensuring that they have all the necessary documentation of medical information for themselves and their loved ones.

■ ***The Inspector*** (Introverted, Sensing, Thinking, and Judging—***ISTJ***). The Inspector, sometimes called the Logistician, is practical and fact based. Their reliability can't be doubted. Inspectors are the pragmatists of the world—hardworking, thorough, and committed to meeting their obligations. They have a no-nonsense rule and will rarely call attention to themselves. Their natural sense of detail leads them to careers in finance, engineering, and medicine. They also do well in supervisor and administrative roles that require quick decision-making. At the social end, Inspectors enjoy computer games, chess, and other board games. Inspectors make up 12% of the population. **Patient advocate perspective:** This patient may need your help the least, as they are very detail oriented. These individuals tend to be thinking patients, meaning that they are actually cognitively processing and applying information like a scientist. Therefore, as a thinking patient, your suggestions to improve their healthcare status would be welcome.

■ ***The Craftsman*** (Introverted, Sensing, Thinking, and Perceiving—***ISTP***). Because the Craftsman is a master of all kinds of tools and a designer of bold and practical experiments, they can also be called Virtuosos. Craftsmen are the handymen of the world, using their technical expertise to solve practical problems. They are excellent troubleshooters. While not likely to share their personal information, they always jump to pitch in wherever they are needed. Their ability to manipulate tools in their environment leads them to careers in information technology (IT) and engineering. With the element of risk, they also choose careers in law enforcement, medicine, or mechanics. Their hobbies can include extreme sports, weaponry, or any work with gadgets. The Craftsman comprises 5% of the population. **Patient advocate perspective:** This patient, being tech savvy, might appreciate online programs or mobile apps to investigate wellness programs, practitioners, or third-party providers.

Patient Advocate Experience: Imagine the following scenario. A healthcare professional who is a millennial (Healer) is working with a family that includes a patient who is part of the Great Generation (Commander), two baby boomer children (Visionary/Craftsman) with healthcare issues themselves, and an MTV generation sibling (Composer).

Lesson Learned: If the millennial healthcare provider, who is naturally a healer, is unable to adapt their message, critical information will not be exchanged among the parties. This is compounded by a failure to recognize the personality traits of the family unit, such as those who are outgoing and in charge versus those who are introverted and will not take charge of a situation. The result will be compounded unmet expectations, confusion, and frustration to poor patient outcomes. The next practice guide will expand the generational status and personality type with basic human emotions.

Chapter 7

PHP Instructors' Guide to Basic Human Emotions

I cannot teach anybody anything, I can only make them think.

Socrates
Greek philosopher

This abstract is a summary of basic human emotions.* Table 7.1 is a summary of human emotional attributes by the various theorists noted. Table 7.2 includes components of emotions noted by Shaver et al. (2001), listing primary, secondary, and tertiary emotions. Simply, these tables provide another perspective for the patient advocate to understand people and the potential impact of core emotions when communicating with them. Recognizing varying emotions can guide and facilitate an understanding of your own reactions and help form responses to each single patient or provider. This reference is provided as an informational supplement to the other guides in this book.

The following are front-line stories categorized by the basic human emotion(s) described in both Tables 7.1 and 7.2. ***People are driven and impacted by the variations of the rawest and most basic human emotions of love, joy, surprise, anger, sadness, and fear.*** Being prepared for and consciously aware of these various emotions can help you to better serve the patient and take advocacy to the next level. Can you identify the emotions in each illustration? Can you anticipate patient/provider reactions when negative or positive events occur? The illustrations highlight the applicable emotions from the theorist perspective (Table 7.1), followed by an illustration of the Shaver emotions. Each illustration provides a suggested response for consideration by the patient advocate.

---

* http://changingminds.org/explanations/emotions/basic%20emotions.htm.

Table 7. 1   (Theorist) Review of Defined Basic Emotions: "Theorist Emotions Identified"

Theorist	Basic Emotions
Plutchik	Acceptance, anger, anticipation, disgust, joy, fear, sadness, surprise
Arnold	Anger, aversion, courage, dejection, desire, despair, fear, hate, hope, love, sadness
Ekman, Friesen, and Ellsworth	Anger, disgust, fear, joy, sadness, surprise
Frijda	Desire, happiness, interest, surprise, wonder, sorrow
Gray	Rage and terror, anxiety, joy
Izard	Anger, contempt, disgust, distress, fear, guilt, interest, joy, shame, surprise
James	Fear, grief, love, rage
McDougall	Anger, disgust, elation, fear, subjection, tender-emotion, wonder
Mowrer	Pain, pleasure
Oatley and Johnson-Laird	Anger, disgust, anxiety, happiness, sadness
Panksepp	Expectancy, fear, rage, panic
Tomkins	Anger, interest, contempt, disgust, distress, fear, joy, shame, surprise
Watson	Fear, love, rage
Weiner and Graham	Happiness, sadness

Source: Ortony, A. and Turner, T. J., *Psychological Review*, 97, 315–331, 1990.

Illustration #1: Provider in Protocol Mode: An Irritated Nurse—A Nervous Patient

A patient in the emergency room (ER) repeatedly reminds his nurse about a chronic condition. She states "I heard you five times. Yes, I know that you are a hemophiliac." The doctor arrives and examines the patient for his complaint of chest pain. The nurse returns and hands the patient aspirin and Ativan. The patient looks at her and states: "Why are you giving this to me?" Her response: "This is our protocol for patients with chest pain." He reminds her, yet again, "I can't take aspirin, I am a hemophiliac!"

Table 7.1 (Theorist) emotions identified: Anger, fear, anxiety, disgust, and panic

Table 7.2 (Shaver) emotions identified:

> ***Patient*** → irritation, frustration, dislike, disappointment, fear, anxiety, and diligence
>
> ***Nurse*** → irritation, annoyance, grouchiness, resentment, tenseness, and negligence

Table 7. 2   (Shaver) Review of Emotions Defined: "Shaver Emotions Identified"

Primary Emotion	Secondary Emotion	Tertiary Emotions
Love	Affection	Adoration, affection, love, fondness, liking, attraction, caring, tenderness, compassion, sentimentality
	Lust	Arousal, desire, lust, passion, infatuation
	Longing	Longing
Joy	Cheerfulness	Amusement, bliss, cheerfulness, gaiety, glee, jolliness, joviality, joy, delight, enjoyment, gladness, happiness, jubilation, elation, satisfaction, ecstasy, euphoria
	Zest	Enthusiasm, zeal, zest, excitement, thrill, exhilaration
	Contentment	Contentment, pleasure
	Pride	Pride, triumph
	Optimism	Eagerness, hope, optimism
	Enthrallment	Enthrallment, rapture
	Relief	Relief
Surprise	Surprise	Amazement, surprise, astonishment
Anger	Irritation	Aggravation, irritation, agitation, annoyance, grouchiness, grumpiness
	Exasperation	Exasperation, frustration
	Rage	Anger, rage, outrage, fury, wrath, hostility, ferocity, bitterness, hate, loathing, scorn, spite, vengefulness, dislike, resentment
	Disgust	Disgust, revulsion, contempt
	Envy	Envy, jealousy
	Torment	Torment
Sadness	Suffering	Agony, suffering, hurt, anguish
	Sadness	Depression, despair, hopelessness, gloom, glumness, sadness, unhappiness, grief, sorrow, woe, misery, melancholy
	Disappointment	Dismay, disappointment, displeasure
	Shame	Guilt, shame, regret, remorse
	Neglect	Alienation, isolation, neglect, loneliness, rejection, homesickness, defeat, dejection, insecurity, embarrassment, humiliation, insult
	Sympathy	Pity, sympathy

(Continued)

Table PHP 7. 2 (*Continued*)   **(Shaver) Review of Emotions Defined: "Shaver Emotions Identified"**

Primary Emotion	Secondary Emotion	Tertiary Emotions
Fear	Horror	Alarm, shock, fear, fright, horror, terror, panic, hysteria, mortification
	Nervousness	Anxiety, nervousness, tenseness, uneasiness, apprehension, worry, distress, dread

Source: Shaver, P., et al., *Emotions in Social Psychology: Essential Readings*, 26–56, Philadelphia, PA, Psychology Press, 2001.

Suggested advocate response:

As an advocate, work with individuals to be conscious of their own emotions, in addition to those of the provider. Be simple and direct—"Nurse, I am concerned because I don't want to receive a medication that adversely affects my blood-clotting time." Encourage patients to keep advocating for themselves and to not worry about the emotional state of the staff. If the staff continue to conduct themselves inappropriately, ask for another caregiver. In this case, the patient's continued self-advocacy averted a serious medical error.

Illustration #2: Arrogant Provider—Distraught Wife

A wife visiting her husband in hospital is overwhelmed to learn about a possible heart surgery, a blood clot in the leg, and the declining condition of her husband's overall health. All three of these scenarios had various life-threatening probabilities. The consulting cardiologist, ordered by the husband's physician, walked into the patient's room and demanded to know why the wife had asked for a second opinion when he had advised them which procedure should be done first. The bewildered wife simply stated, "I just don't know what to do!" The doctor paused, glared at the wife and said, "By the way, your husband has cancer too," and stormed out of the room.

Table 7.1 (Theorist) emotions identified: Anger, fear, anxiety, despair, and distress

Table 7.2 (Shaver) emotions identified:

Wife → surprise, exasperation, anger, contempt, anguish, sadness, grief, panic, and desperation
Physician → anger, contempt, impatience, bitterness, scorn, resentment, and spite

Suggested advocate response: In a situation in which a patient feels threatened or uncomfortable during a hospital visit, the first thing they must do is ask if the hospital has a patient advocate program and to request a visit from its staff. They will help monitor any further complications involved. In this case, a compliance officer did get involved and the physician was prohibited from further contact with the family.

Illustration #3: Anguished Provider—Despairing Patient

A cancer doctor received notice (after receipt of an FDA notice) that the facility to which had he sent a patient for chemotherapy had inadvertently purchased a counterfeit chemotherapy treatment inventory. The facility had tracked down all the patients that had received this inventory and had contacted the prescribing physician. The physician had to explain to an early-stage diagnosed breast cancer patient, who had now progressed to stage 4, why the chemotherapy did not work and that she had never received the real drug. The devastated patient lost hope, refused any additional treatment, and died 1 month later.

Table 7.1 (Theorist) emotions: Acceptance, sadness, surprise, anger, grief, disgust, rage, and guilt

Table 7.2 (Shaver) emotions:

> ***Patient*** → frustration, contempt, hurt, anguish, despair and dread, somberness, and loss
>
> ***Physician*** → remorse, pity, sympathy, fury, disappointment, embarrassment, resentment, and regret

Suggested advocate response: This is, sadly, a no-win situation. The immediate reaction is to get the patient and her family into appropriate counseling. Effective education is important, for patients as well as providers, when it comes to the dark sides of healthcare waste, fraud, and abuse (WFA). This is an example of why it is important to have an educational program on how to look for signs of counterfeit medication or adulterated (tampered with) product. WFA risk analysis should be part of any annual review program.

Illustration #4: Fearless Wife—Compassionate Physician

Upon receiving a diagnosis of lung cancer with a life expectancy of 3 months, a mother began researching her medical condition. Within 1 week, she had amassed more information on the subject than her physician. This mother had repeatedly queried her physician as to why she was being recommended chemotherapy as opposed to other drugs and regimens. In the end, her doctor could not articulate why. What was happening was that the doctor was following a defined protocol that was influenced by what the payer would pay. This exemplifies the dangers of a protocol-driven environment versus a data-driven one. Following this incident, the mother's physician worked with her to modify the treatment based on the research provided. Of interest was the receptivity of the doctor to fluctuate between the roles of student, teacher, and advocate. Three years later, the mother is still with us, having become a fully empowered, data-driven patient, blending Eastern and Western medicine into her plan of care. This is the future of healthcare—patients taking control of their health.

Table 7.1 (Theorist) emotions identified: Fear, surprise, wonder, sorrow, distress, joy, and happiness

Table 7.2 (Shaver) emotions identified:

> *Patient*→ satisfaction, triumph, optimism, self-empowerment, and awareness
>
> *Physician* → frustration, hope, compassion, caring, satisfaction, and pride

Suggested advocate response: This is a great example of how all patients should conduct themselves. Healthcare is struggling with how to interact with the patient as a customer. In the meantime, advocates should encourage patients to gather and validate the data on their health. If they hear a response to a question that is not clear, repeat the question. If the response remains vague and unclear, get a second opinion.

Illustration #5: Cocky Doctor—Disgusted Patient

A patient had been recommended to undergo an MRI scan following a visit to her chiropractor in order to assess what was wrong with her knee. After the scan, she met with another doctor to review the results. The doctor told the woman that he did not need to physically read the MRI results, as a visual inspection of her knee by him would suffice. His rationale was that chiropractors were not real doctors and that the scan was unnecessary. "You mean to tell me you are not going to look at the results and will make a recommendation without my report?" The encounter abruptly ended with no payment for the visit, the logic being that if a proper assessment was unnecessary, then neither was his payment. The doctor was later discharged.

Table 7.1 (Theorist) emotions identified: Surprise, anger, disgust, and contempt

Table 7.2 (Shaver) emotions identified:

> *Patient*→ aggravation, vengefulness, resentment, and insult
>
> *Physician* → aggravation, hostility, shock, immaturity, and indolence

Suggested advocate response: This patient immediately lost confidence in her doctor. Once trust and confidence are gone, the best situation is to seek professional guidance from another physician. As patients learn to become empowered in managing their healthcare, expect to see physicians like the one in this example phased out by attrition or loss of customers.

Patient Advocate Experience: Imagine the following scenario. An irritable, angry healthcare professional is going through a divorce and is a millennial (Healer) working with a family that includes a patient who is part of the Great Generation (Commander) and in nervous fear mode pending the results of healthcare tests, two baby boomer children (a Visionary optimist and a Craftsman who is feeling ashamed for not disclosing a recent loss of employment) with healthcare issues themselves, and a happy, zesty MTV generation sibling (Composer) who is thrilled to have gotten a new job.

Lesson Learned: The millennial healthcare provider, who is naturally a Healer, must recognize whether personal issues are impacting their ability to adapt and assess the advocacy message and process critical information that will impact any final recommendations. This is compounded by recipients of information that may not be able to recognize compromised advice, following which they are to make healthcare decisions. This is further impacted by a failure to incorporate the personality traits of the family unit throughout the consultation process. For example, as stated previously, who in the family unit is in charge, who will be the scribe of health information being provided? Who will validate the information to ensure that it is complete and accurate? Are the assignments among the family members appropriately suited for the introverts versus the extroverts in the group? Again, the result will be compounded by unmet expectations, confusion, frustration, and poor patient outcomes. The next practice guide will provide illustrative resources that may be relied upon by all stakeholders.

References

Ekman, P. (1972). Universals and cultural differences in facial expression of emotion. In J. Cole (Ed.), *Nebraska Symposium on Motivation*, 207–283. Lincoln, NE: University of Nebraska Press.

Ekman, P., Friesen, W. V., and Ellsworth, P. (1982). What emotion categories or dimensions can observers judge from facial behavior? In P. Ekman (Ed.), *Emotion in the Human Face*, 39–55. New York: Cambridge University Press.

Frijda, N. H. (1986). *The Emotions*. New York: Cambridge University Press.

Gray, J. A. (1985). The whole and its parts: Behaviour, the brain, cognition and emotion. *Bulletin of the British Psychological Society*, 38, 99–112.

Izard, C. E. (1977). *Human Emotions*. New York: Plenum Press.

Jack, R. E., Garrod, O. G. B., and Schyns, P. G. (2014). Dynamic facial expressions of emotion transmit an evolving hierarchy of signals over time. *Current Biology*, 24, 2, 187–192.

James, W. (1884). What is an emotion? *Mind*, 9, 188–205.

McDougall, W. (1926). *An Introduction to Social Psychology*. Boston: Luce.

Mowrer, O. H. (1960). *Learning Theory and Behavior*. New York: Wiley.

Oatley, K., and Johnson-Laird, P. N. (1987). Towards a cognitive theory of emotions. *Cognition & Emotion*, 1, 29–50.

Ortony, A., and Turner, T. J. (1990). What's basic about basic emotions? *Psychological Review*, 97, 315–331.

Panksepp, J. (1982). Toward a general psychobiological theory of emotions. *The Behavioral and Brain Sciences*, 5, 407–467.

Parrott, W. (2001). *Emotions in Social Psychology*. Philadelphia, PA: Psychology Press.

Plutchik, R. (1980). A general psychoevolutionary theory of emotion. In R. Plutchik and H. Kellerman (Eds.), *Emotion: Theory, Research, and Experience*: Vol. 1. *Theories of Emotion*, 3–33. New York: Academic.

Shaver, P., Schwartz, J., Kirson, D., and O'Connor, C. (2001). Emotional knowledge: Further exploration of a prototype approach. In G. Parrott (Ed.), *Emotions in Social Psychology: Essential Readings*, 26–56. Philadelphia, PA: Psychology Press.

Tomkins, S. S. (1984). Affect theory. In K. R. Scherer and P. Ekman (Eds.), *Approaches to Eemotion*, 163–195. Hillsdale, NJ: Erlbaum.

Watson, J. B. (1930). *Behaviorism*. Chicago: University of Chicago Press.

Weiner, B., and Graham, S. (1984). An attributional approach to emotional development. In C. E. Izard, J. Kagan, and R. B. Zajonc (Eds.), *Emotions, Cognition, and Behavior*, 167–191. New York: Cambridge University Press.

Chapter 8

PHP Instructors' Guide to Illustrative Resources

You treat a disease: You win, you lose. You treat a person, I guarantee you win—no matter the outcome.

Patch Adams
American physician, comedian, social activist

Introduction

The following are illustrative examples of resources that may be utilized by patients and patient advocates in managing their healthcare. Any resources listed are illustrative and do not represent an endorsement; neither is it a comprehensive list. As with any decision, execute due diligence with any organization(s) that may be helpful. Check references and ask for any deliverables to be defined.

Critical Questions Regarding Any Patient Advocacy Resource

- Make sure that you understand who the organization is and how they classify themselves. For example, is it government-sponsored, privately-held, for-profit, or not-for-profit?
- Request all demographic information such as
  - Name and address.
  - Phone numbers.
  - What is their mission?
  - Who sponsors the organization?
  - What credentials do they have?
  - Are they a "for-profit" or "not-for-profit" organization?

– Are they affiliated with any organization?
– Do they have an online presence? If so, what is the Internet address (URL)?
  • Note: Do not assume that the address of a web page followed by .org indicates that an organization is a not-for-profit entity.

Professional Resources: How to Find Them and What to Ask

This is the era of the consumer. Along with this are ongoing roles and support that are being introduced to help consumers. If you retain a resource, ask for its credentials, experience, and licenses. Each state has a Department of Professional Regulation that will validate a license and/or look for any related disciplinary issues. The Better Business Bureau is another tool available to research the background of any organization. The following list provides various examples of support groups for individuals:

■ **Advocacy Groups (For Profit):** Groups staffed by healthcare professionals, financial advisers, or lawyers to help patients coordinate or fund their care.
■ **Advocacy Groups (Nonprofit):** Mission-driven, philanthropic, and/or grant-funded organizations.
■ **Decision-Making Advocates:** These advocates help patients make their best personal medical choices based on the patient's own values and beliefs. A similar service is healthcare mediation—helping families decide on the best medical care for a debilitated loved one.
■ **Financial Advocates—Money and Health:** Medical bills and claim reviewers help people sort through their medical bills, determine if the bills are indeed correct, and even negotiate for them with hospitals, doctors, or vendors who have charged them in error.
■ **Health Exchange or Marketplace Navigators:** These navigators help patients choose the right health insurance plan to satisfy the ACA (Affordable Care Act) individual mandate or any other legislative changes that are made on any healthcare requirements.
■ **Health Coaching Advocates:** Health coaches concentrate on wellness. Many employers and insurance providers are promoting healthy, improved lifestyle choices using education and motivation.
■ **Patient Advocates in Hospitals:** Often belonging to the American Hospital Association (AHA), hospital advocates provide assistance for patients or family members when they run into problems during or after their hospital stay. These problems can relate to care or paying for that care. Patients may seek help for anything from getting a ride home from the hospital to having a medical bill explained.
■ **Patient Advocates:** Individual practitioners and professional or nonprofessional healthcare assistants who build their careers on helping patients

navigate the healthcare system and make good personal health decisions. This navigation includes anything from organizing personal health portfolios and providing bill tracking and payment assistance to providing support when older patients transition into assisted living and nursing homes.

- **Professional Practice Development Resources:** The **Patient Advocate** industry is evolving at a fast pace. Look for professional groups that are developing patient advocates. In addition, stay current within your respective area of expertise. For example, if you are a billing expert, stay current on the appropriate credentials for your discipline.

Professional Organizations: How to Find Them and What to Ask

Practice standards are constantly evolving. With rapid changes in technology and the amount of data being generated, professionals need to seek out continuous education in order to stay current. It is important to ask your advocate which practice standards they apply and where they obtain their ongoing education. Many niche areas will have specific professional associations. The following is an illustrative listing of professional support groups and subject matter expert resources.

- **American Health Information Management Association (AHIMA):** A professional organization for the field of effective management of health data and medical records needed to deliver quality healthcare to public management (www.ahima.org).
- **Association of Certified Fraud Examiners (ACFE):** The professional organization that governs fraud examiners. Activities include producing fraud information, tools, and training (www.acfe.com).
- **Association of Healthcare Internal Auditors (AHIA):** A network of experienced healthcare internal auditing professionals who come together to share tools, knowledge, and insight on how to assess and evaluate risk within a complex and dynamic healthcare environment (www.ahia.org).
- **Case Management Society of America (CMSA):** The leading membership association providing professional collaboration across the healthcare continuum to advocate for patients' well-being and improved health outcomes by fostering case management growth and development, impacting healthcare policy, and providing evidence-based tools and resources (www.cmsa.org).
- **Data Management Association (DAMA):** A not-for-profit, vendor-independent, international association of technical and business professionals dedicated to advancing the concepts and practices of information resource management and data resource management (www.dama.org).
- **Healthcare Billing and Management Association (HBMA):** Committed to advancing the healthcare billing and management industry through

advocacy and by providing education, information, and other valuable resources to its members while promoting high ethical and professional standards (www.hbma.org).

■ **Healthcare Financial Management Association (HFMA):** A nonprofit membership organization for healthcare financial management executives (www.hfma.org).

■ **International Association of Rehabilitation Professionals (IARP):** The premier global association for professionals involved in private rehabilitation. Leaders in case and disability management, forensics, vocational expertise, and life-care planning are members of this community, known for its diversity, mentoring, entrepreneurial approach, and intellectual power (www.rehabpro.org).

■ **National Patient Advocate Foundation:** Affiliate of the Patient Advocate Foundation. Provides information on legislative updates. Advocates for individuals suffering a chronic debilitating or life-threatening condition (www.npaf.org).

■ **Patient Advocate Foundation:** Focused on solving insurance and healthcare access problems. The Patient Advocate Foundation's patient services provide patients with arbitration, mediation, and negotiation to settle issues with access to care, medical debt, and job retention related to their illness (www.patientadvocate.org).

Government-Sponsored Organizations: How to Find Them and What to Ask

Federal resources may be found through the listings of various healthcare organizations and professional associations. At the state level, reviewing their respective web sites under "agencies" will often direct an individual to available resources within that state. State government resources such as the Office of Patient Advocacy in New York or the Office of the Patient Advocate in California have established programs to protect patient rights and ensure that medical services are delivered consistent with regulations and expected standards. Search the Internet for "Office of Patient Advocate," "Office of Healthcare Advocate," and so on, to see if your state has any type of patient advocate support. Note that the Centers for Medicaid and Medicare Services (CMS) provide a current listing of patient rights at the federal level.

Federal Resources

■ **CMS**
  – Patient's Bill of Rights
  – Consumer support information
  – Content requirements for plan finder
  – Preexisting condition insurance plan
  – Other current guidance
  – www.cms.gov

- **Agency for Healthcare Research and Quality (AHRQ)**
  - The AHRQ oversees research on healthcare quality, costs, outcomes, and patient safety
  - www.ahrq.gov
- **Centers for Disease Control (CDC)**
  - The CDC is charged with protecting the health of Americans
  - www.cdc.gov
- **Food and Drug Administration (FDA)**
  - Regulates various industries that focus on the foods and medicines we consume
  - Provides an overview of all approved medications
  - Publishes a listing of any drug or product recalls
  - Provides notice of any counterfeit products found
  - www.fda.gov
- **Institute of Medicine (IOM)**
  - The IOM is a component of the National Academies of Sciences and, while most consider it a part of the government, it has the distinction of working outside the framework of the government to provide background for policy development.
  - www.cdc.gov
- **National Institute of Health (NIH)**
  - The NIH is a national medical research agency supporting scientific studies.
  - www.nih.gov
- **U.S. Department of Health and Human Services (HHS)**
  - The Health Insurance Portability and Accountability Act (HIPAA) and your health rights
  - Health insurance
  - Social services
  - Prevention and wellness
  - Complaints and appeals
  - Other current guidance
  - www.hhs.gov
- **Healthcare Fraud Prevention and Enforcement Action Team (HEAT) Provider Compliance Training**
  - Free videos and audio podcasts (averaging about 4 minutes each) covering major healthcare fraud and abuse laws, the basics of healthcare compliance programs, and what to do when a compliance issue arises. This is part of the Office of the Inspector General (OIG)'s award-winning HEAT provider compliance training initiative.
  - http://oig.hhs.gov/compliance/provider-compliance-training/
- **OIG: COMPLIANCE**
  - **Compliance 101 and Provider Education**
    - The OIG developed the free educational resources listed on its Compliance 101 web page to help healthcare providers, practitioners,

and suppliers to understand the healthcare fraud and abuse laws and the consequences of violating them.

- **Accountable Care Organizations**
  - The Affordable Care Act contains several provisions that support the development of accountable care organizations to manage and coordinate care for beneficiaries.
- **Compliance Guidance**
  - The OIG has developed a series of voluntary compliance program guidance documents directed at various segments of the healthcare industry.
  - http://oig.hhs.gov/compliance/

■ **OIG: FRAUD**

- **Child Support Enforcement**
  - Parents who fail to pay court-ordered child support for the care of their children put an unnecessary strain on the custodial parent and the children, as well as on agencies that are tasked with enforcing these matters. Although most child support cases fall under state jurisdiction, the OIG plays an important role in aggressively pursuing parents who fail to pay court-ordered child support.
- **Consumer Alerts**
  - To protect individuals from criminals attempting to steal money from you or the government.
- **Enforcement Actions**
  - The OIG and other state and federal agencies collaborate to ensure civil, criminal, and/or administrative action is taken against providers who break the laws governing federal healthcare programs.
  - http://oig.hhs.gov/fraud/

State Resources

Each state may have a variety of resources available to the patient advocate in addition to individual consumers. Categories to search for include any legislation involving patient rights, medical identity theft, privacy, and/or access rights. If you have a minor or older person as a client, also search for attributes involving elder rights in addition to the rights of minor children.

Each state typically will have a state department of insurance, a department of professional regulation to look up licenses, and a state department of public health, in addition to a county-specific health department and various consumer hotlines.

Another evolving area of interest is data portals that states are beginning to develop to allow consumers access to other online public data as part of transparency initiatives and/or online accessibility for citizens. The following is an illustration for the State of Illinois.

- **Illustrative Example: Illinois**
  - **Applicable Legislation**
    - The Fair Patient Billing Act (Source: P.A. 94-885, eff. 1-1-07.)
    - Sample requirements
      - Patient notification requirements
      - Bill information requirements
      - Bill inquiry requirements
      - Application procedures for financial assistance
      - http://www.ilga.gov/legislation/ilcs/ilcs3. asp?ActID=2798&ChapterID=21
  - **Department of Professional Regulation**
    - Illinois Department of Financial and Professional Regulation
    - Public resource to look up and validate professional licenses
    - www.idpfr.com
  - **Department of Public Health**
    - Illinois Department of Public Health (IDPH)
    - www.dph.illinios.gov
  - **Department of County Health**
    - County example: Cook County Public Health
    - www.cookcountypublichealth.org
  - **State Department of Insurance**
    - Illinois Department of Insurance
      - http://insurance.illinois.gov/
  - **Open Data Portals**
    - State of Illinois Open Data Portal Initiative
    - IDPH Home Health Agency Directory
    - IDPH Hospice Directory
    - Provide Data
    - Numerous public data on health, housing, labor, Medicaid, municipality, and so forth
    - https://data.illinois.gov/
  - **See your state's website for more resources**

A similar process of using Internet searches for finding similar resources with the State of New York. Each link will take you to the specific criteria offered by that state-specific program.

- **Illustrative Example: New York**
  - **Applicable Legislation**
    - "Emergency Medical Services and Surprise Bills"
      - Sources for bill: http://assembly.state.ny.us/leg/?default_fld=&bn=A0 9205&term=2013&Summary=Y&Text=Y

     ◾ https://www.mintz.com/newsletter/2015/
      Advisories/4872-0415-NAT-HL/

- Ensures that consumers who receive unexpected bills pay no more than their usual in-network cost sharing and/or copayment amounts, regardless of the network status of the treating physician
- Mandates greater transparency obligations on the part of providers and health plans regarding out-of-network (OON) charges and network participation
- Incorporates broader rights for a patient to go OON if the insurance plan's existing network is insufficient

  – **Department of Professional Regulation**
- See State listing of resources
- http://www.op.nysed.gov/

  – **Department of Public Health**
- See State listing of resources
- https://www.health.ny.gov/

  – **Department of County Health**
- See State listing of resources
- https://www.health.ny.gov/contact/contact_information/

  – **State Department of Insurance**
- See State listing of resources
- http://www.dfs.ny.gov/insurance/dfs_insurance.htm

  – **Open Data Portals**
- See State listing of resources
- https://nycopendata.socrata.com/

  – **See your state's website for more resources**
- See State listing of resources
- http://www.newyork.com/

■ **Illustrative Example: California**

  – **Applicable Legislation**
- See State listing of resources
- https://s3.amazonaws.com/s3.documentcloud.org/documents/2094229/533.pdf (this bill has recently been introduced and is pending further review; however, it is applicable to billing)

  – **Department of Professional Regulation**
- See State listing of resources
- http://www.dca.ca.gov/

  – **Department of Public Health**
- See State listing of resources
- http://www.cdph.ca.gov/Pages/DEFAULT.aspx

  – **Department of County Health**
- See State listing of resources
- https://www.cdph.ca.gov/programs/immunize/pages/californialocalhealthdepartments.aspx

- **State Department of Insurance**
  - See State listing of resources
  - http://www.insurance.ca.gov/
- **Open Data Portals**
  - See State listing of resources
  - https://chhs.data.ca.gov/
- **See your state's website for more resources**

Legislative References

Federal and state legislation may be helpful in understanding patient rights and other access-to-care considerations. The following is an illustrative listing of potential sources and sponsor organizations that attempt to aggregate legislative information at a state and federal level.

- ■ **Health information and the law: Sample resources to find current privacy rights by state**
  - While there are a number of federal laws governing privacy and access to individual health information, most states have enacted their own laws and regulations pertaining to the use, collection, and disclosure of health information (http://www.healthinfolaw.org/state).
  - Offers information on each state what their laws pertain to for the privacy of patients (https://patientprivacyrights.org/privacy-laws-by-state/).
  - The Harmonizing State Privacy Law Collaborative was formed to (1) develop processes and tools for states to use to work toward harmonizing disparate state laws, and (2) provide a framework for a coordinated approach among states to ensure that when states approach health information technology (IT)-related reforms, they do not codify new or current variations that could make nationwide electronic health information exchange more difficult (https://www.healthit.gov/policy-researchers-implementers/harmonizing-state-privacy-law).
- ■ **Immunization laws for healthcare workers and patients**
  - One tool used to maintain low rates of vaccine-preventable disease is vaccination law. State vaccination laws include vaccination requirements for children in public and private schools and daycare settings, college/university students, and healthcare workers and patients in certain facilities (http://www.cdc.gov/phlp/publications/topic/vaccinationlaws.html).
- ■ **Information on state medical record laws**
  - Medical records confidentiality laws outline patients' rights to the privacy of their medical information and the circumstances under which that information may (or must) be disclosed. Each state is listed to show what

the law is for that particular state (http://statelaws.findlaw.com/healthcare-laws/medical-records.html).

Support Groups and Resource Organizations: How to Find Them and What to Ask

A good place to start is to ask your provider for any resources they have utilized in the past. Often, county and state government web sites may have listings as well. Use key words like "association" paired with the specific topic "cancer," for example, to find helpful organizations. As mentioned earlier, always apply due diligence and consult your provider. Please note that the volume of resources is so extensive that online support peer-to-peer group communities such as **online.supportgroups.com** (over 3 million resources) are being organized. The following are illustrative examples.

Disease Support Organizations—Key word search: Name of disease or condition, association, support, society

- **Alzheimer's Association**
  The Alzheimer's Association national site provides information on Alzheimer's disease and dementia symptoms, diagnosis, stages, treatment, care, and support resources (www.alz.org).
- **American Brain Foundation**
  The American Brain Foundation supports vital research and education to discover causes, improved treatments, and cures for brain and other nervous system diseases (www.americanbrainfoundation.org).
- **American Cancer Society**
  Dedicated to helping persons who face cancer. Supports research, patient services, early detection, treatment, and education (www.cancer.org).
- **American Diabetes Association**
  The mission of this organization is to prevent and cure diabetes and to improve the lives of all people affected by this disease (www.diabetes.org).
- **American Disability Foundation**
  Specializing in disability advocacy, this organization was founded to address the critical issues of poverty resulting from mental and physical disabilities that often resulted in widespread homelessness (http://adisability.org/).
- **American Foundation of Suicide Prevention**
  A small group of caring individuals with a vision: to establish a private source of support for suicide research and education and to ensure that essential suicide prevention efforts could be sustained into the future (http://afsp.org/).
- **American Heart Association**
  This association looks to reduce the number of deaths caused by **heart** disease and stroke (www.heart.org).

■ **American Liver Foundation**

The American Liver Foundation's goal is to facilitate, advocate, and promote education, support, and research for the prevention, treatment, and cure of liver disease (www.liverfoundation.org).

■ **Civitan Foundation**

Civitan provides communities with an accessible, safe, and affordable environment while delivering superior life experiences to enhance the quality of life among individuals with developmental disabilities of all ages (www.civitanfoundationaz.com).

■ **National Kidney Foundation**

The National Kidney Foundation is the leading organization in the United States dedicated to the awareness, prevention, and treatment of kidney disease for hundreds of thousands of healthcare professionals, millions of patients and their families, and tens of millions of Americans at risk (www.kidney.org).

■ **National Multiple Sclerosis Society**

This society is united in its collective power to do something about multiple sclerosis now to end this disease forever (www.nationalmssociety.org).

■ **National Organization for Rare Disorders (NORD)**

Information about this organization, its programs and special events, and its variety of services is offered. It includes a rare disease and orphan drug database (www.rarediseases.org).

■ **Penn Foundation Behavioral Health Services**

Provides compassionate, responsive, and innovative care that addresses the mental health, substance use, and intellectual disability needs of the community (www.pennfoundation.org).

■ **Skin Cancer Foundation**

The Skin Cancer Foundation has set the standard for educating the public and the medical profession about skin cancer, its prevention by means of sun protection, the need for early detection, and prompt, effective treatment (www.skincancer.org).

Understanding Healthcare Reimbursement: How to Find It and What to Ask

The market has both public, private, for-profit, and nonprofit organizations that accumulate financial healthcare information. This includes resources that provide support in understanding the coding systems that are used to represent conditions to report healthcare services. Regardless of the source, always validate the organization, its sponsors, and the source of its data. A list of billing/coding/financial organizations can be found below.

■ **American Hospital Directory**

The American Hospital Directory provides operational data, financial information, utilization statistics, and other benchmarks for acute care hospitals (https://www.ahd.com).

■ **American Academy of Professional Coders (AAPC)**
Provides education and professional certification to physician-based medical coders and elevates the standards of medical coding by providing student training, certification, ongoing education, networking, and job opportunities (http://www.aapc.com/).

■ **American Association of Medical Audit Specialists (AAMAS)**
Provides resources and support to advance the practice of medical auditing (http://www.aamas.org/).

■ **American College of Medical Coding Specialists (ACMCS)**
A new, not-for-profit professional coder's organization developed solely for its members. Your voice drives the organization. You are the organization. We need your thoughts, suggestions, needs, and support to make the organization the best it can be (https://www.acmcs.org/).

■ **American Institute of Certified Public Accountants (AICPA)**
The *AICPA Core Competency Framework*, developed by educators for educators, defines a set of skills-based competencies needed by all students entering the accounting profession, regardless of the career path they choose (public/industry/government/nonprofit) or the specific accounting services they will perform (http://www.aicpa.org/interestareas/accountingeducation/resources/pages/corecompetency.aspx).

■ **American Medical Billing Association (AMBA)**
Provides industry and regulatory education and networking opportunities for its members to be able to share information and ideas and to market member's abilities and professional services as a group (http://www.ambanet.net/AMBA.htm).

■ **Applicable State Workers Compensation Fee Schedules**
– Illustrative example: State of Illinois
  • Illinois Workers' Compensation Commission
  • The fee schedule applies to medical treatments and procedures that are rendered on or after February 1, 2006, and are covered under Section 8 of the Illinois Workers' Compensation Act. The fees are calculated according to the criteria set forth in Section 8.2 of the Act. Payment for medical care covered under the Act shall be the lesser of the healthcare provider's actual charge or the fee schedule amount. If, however, the employer/insurer and healthcare provider enter into a contract for different reimbursement levels, they would follow the contract instead of the fee schedule (https://iwcc.ingenix.com).

■ **Certification Commission for Healthcare Interpreters (CCHI)**
A comprehensive credentialing program for healthcare interpreters that brings together representatives from national and regional nonprofit interpreting associations, language companies, community-based organizations, educational institutions, healthcare providers, and advocates for limited English proficiency (LEP) individuals. Serves the current and future needs of

healthcare interpreters and stakeholders (healthcare providers and institutions, language services agencies, government agencies, and patients) who are counting on the organization to provide a trained, qualified, certified, and competency-based population of healthcare interpreters (http://www.healthcareinterpretercertification.org/certification/apply-now/143.html).

■ **Coding Institute (The), LLC**
Dedicated to offering quality products and services to help healthcare organizations succeed. Primarily focused on providing specialty-specific content, code sets, continuing education opportunities, consulting services, and a supportive community of healthcare professionals and experts (http://www.codinginstitute.com/).

■ **Craneware**
Leader in automated revenue integrity solutions that improve the financial performance of healthcare organizations (http://www.craneware.com).

■ **Fairhealth**
Fairhealth is a national, independent, not-for-profit corporation whose mission is to bring transparency to healthcare costs and health insurance information (www.fairhealth.org).

■ **Financial Accounting Standards Board (FASB)**
The FASB Accounting Standards Codification® is the source of authoritative and generally accepted accounting principles (GAAP) recognized by FASB as applicable to nongovernmental entities. *Presentation and Disclosure of Patient Service Revenue, Provision for Bad Debts*, and the *Allowance for Doubtful Accounts for Certain Healthcare Entities* (http://www.fasb.org/cs/BlobServer?blobcol=urldata&blobtable=MungoBlobs&blobkey=id&blobwhere=1175822797036&blobheader=application/pdf).

■ **Florida Medical Auditors Association (FMAA)**
The objective of FMAA is to
  – Develop and promote an environment conducive to the open exchange of information pertinent to medical auditing
  – Develop and create acceptance of criterion, which fosters professional performance by the individual medical auditor and their approach to the field of medical auditing
  – Create an open exchange of information between the healthcare provider, the third-party payer, and the medical auditor regarding the philosophy, the audit process, and the outcome
  – http://www.floridamedicalauditorsassociation.org/index.htm
Good Rx
Compares retail prices of prescription drugs from different pharmacies across the United States (www.**goodrx**.com)

■ **Healthcare Billing and Management Association (HBMA)**
Committed to advancing the healthcare billing and management industry through advocacy and by providing education, information, and other

valuable resources to its members while promoting high ethical and professional standards (http://www.hbma.org/).

■ **Healthcare Interpreter Certificate Program**
A curriculum designed to train bilingual and bicultural students to develop their awareness, knowledge, and skills necessary for effective language interpretation in healthcare settings (http://www.ccsf.edu).

■ **Healthcare Finance Certified Specialist Programs**
Mastering Healthcare Accounting and Finance is an *Advanced Technical Study Certificate Program* offering an overview of accounting and finance processes used in healthcare provider organizations (http://www.hfma.org).

■ **Medical Codes: Frequently Asked Questions**
This web site offers links to various types of medical codes (http://www.nlm.nih.gov/services/medcodes.html).

■ **Medicare Payment Advisory Commission**
An important resource that provides Congress with nonpartisan analysis and policy advice on the Medicare program. Within this site is a specific section referred to as "payment basics." This section provides an overview of how certain types of services are paid for. For example, a briefing is provided on how ambulatory surgical center services payment systems are formulated (http://www.medpac.gov/-documents-/payment-basics).

■ **Medicare Provider Analysis and Review Data**
These files contain information on Medicare beneficiaries using hospital inpatient services. The data are provided by the state and the diagnosis-related groups for all short-stay and inpatient hospitals for the fiscal years 2005–2007 (https://www.cms.gov).

■ **MT Desk: Medical Transcription Style Guide and Reference**
A style guide for medical transcriptionists, healthcare documentation specialists, and health information managers. On completion, this wiki-style guide will be compatible with the current accepted medical transcription style guide but will be dynamically updated to incorporate the most recent information, pictures and illustrations, and comments from the medical transcription and health information community (http://www.mtdesk.com).

■ **National Council on Interpreting Healthcare (NCIHC)**
A multidisciplinary organization whose mission is to promote and enhance language access in healthcare in the United States. The group is composed of leaders from around the country who work as medical interpreters, interpreter service coordinators and trainers, clinicians, policymakers, advocates, and researchers (http://www.ncihc.org/).

■ **National CPA Healthcare Advisors Association (HCAA)**
A nationwide network of certified public accountant (CPA) firms devoted to serving the healthcare industry. Members are selected for their experience and ability to provide proactive solutions to the accounting needs of physicians and physician groups (http://www.hcaa.com/public/default.asp).

- **National Fee Analyzer Book**
Charge data for evaluating fees nationally.
- **Physicians Products**
Offers unique, turn-key services to boost physicians' practice and income. Its services produce new revenue streams that patients are willing to pay out of pocket, and very little extra equipment is needed. It enables physician practices to thrive with the support of specialized and proven management solutions (http://www.physiciansproducts.net).
- **Professional Edition CPT (Current Procedural Terminology) Book**
CPT codebook with rules and guidelines.
- **Supercoder**
Online medical coding tool that makes it easy to look up CPT, healthcare common procedure coding system (HCPCS), and International Classification of Diseases (ICD)-9 and -10 codes, and offers the most extensive collection of coding, billing, compliance, and reimbursement tools (https://www.**supercoder**.com).

Educational Resources for Parents: How to Find Them and What to Ask

Managing and raising children with some type of health and educational need can be overwhelming. Numerous types of support exist, including a niche advocate that is experienced in working with families who have special needs children in the school system. The following is an illustrative listing of the support available.

- **The Center for Parenting Education:** A resource to help educate and support parents to foster confidence, responsibility, and compassion in their children. The center offers a multitude of resources, both on the Internet and in person, and presents the information on its web site as a service to Internet users (http://centerforparentingeducation.org).
- **EDUTOPIA:** List of articles, videos, and other resources to help parents engage productively with their children's teachers and school (http://www.edutopia.org/parent-leadership-education-resources).
- **Learning Disabilities Association of America:** Resources for parents advocating for their children in school and for themselves at work (http://ldaamerica.org).
- **National Center for Learning Disabilities:** Empowering parents and young adults to advocate for equal rights and opportunities. Online resources and community help people to gain the academic, social, and emotional skills needed to succeed in school, at work, and in life (http://www.ncld.org/mission-and-history).

- **AdLit.Org Adolescent Literacy:** A national multimedia project offering information and resources to the parents of struggling adolescent readers and writers at grades 4–12. AdLit.org is an educational initiative of *WETA*, the flagship public television and radio station in the nation's capital, and is funded by the Carnegie Corporation of New York and by the Ann B. and Thomas L. Friedman Family Foundation (http://www.adlit.org).
- **Center for Parent Information and Resources:** Serves as a central resource of information and products focusing on serving families of children with disabilities. A centralized hub of resources, webinars, and publications (http://www.parentcenterhub.org).
- **Jumpstart:** Educational resources for parents to make the process of learning easier and more fun. Parents can find supplementary material that will help them be part of their children's learning. There are suggestions for activities and educational games that parents can do with their children (http://www.jumpstart.com).
- **Discovery Education:** Offers a variety of free family resources and relevant material for parents and their children. Other resources that are vetted by Discovery Education are designed with parents in mind (http://www.discoveryeducation.com).
- **PBS Parents**: A resource that's filled with information on child development and early learning, offering access to educational games and activities inspired by the PBS KIDS programs (http://www.pbs.org/parents).

Patient Advocate Experience: The diversity of healthcare consumer experience is tremendous in both scope and breadth. The pace of technology balanced accelerated innovation and ongoing political client creates challenges for both the advocate and the consumer. It is important to create a strategy and understand your focus as an advocate.

Lesson Learned: A patient advocate practice should include a strategy for continuing education, keeping current on latest technology.

PATIENT ADVOCACY INSTRUCTOR MATERIALS

If you are planning for a year, sow rice; if you are planning for a decade, plant trees; if you are planning for a lifetime, educate people.

Chinese proverb

The next six chapters provide specific material to consider when providing individuals with a 360 degree perspective on navigating the healthcare system. They include learning objectives, content material, and study questions.

This series of Personal Healthcare Portfolio (PHP) instruction guides begins with a discussion on providing an overview of the healthcare problem. It highlights examples of issues and risks faced by all stakeholders. This includes patients, providers, employers, payers, and other vendors within healthcare.

The following PHP instruction materials are focused on how to use a PHP. In essence, an individual cannot effectively manage their health without all of their information. In addition, a professional cannot be effective in the role of a patient advocate without a complete picture of that individual's health status. In the course of collecting materials for the portfolio, it is important to understand the roadblocks a patient may encounter. So, the second set of PHP instructions will illustrate information that is important to understand the vulnerabilities in healthcare.

The PHP instructor materials on personal health information provide insight on how to actually obtain and collect health information. Sample forms to obtain health information are included. This chapter includes guidance on how to ensure the information is accurate, as well as other privacy considerations.

The PHP instructor materials on personal health finances include a discussion on how to collect billing and reimbursement information. General materials on managing both personal and healthcare finance are included.

The PHP instructor materials on buyer beware summarize how to protect your health information in addition to illustrating examples of how your personal health information can be exploited and what can be done with it.

Chapter 9

PHP Instructor Materials: Overview of the Healthcare "Problem"

Education is what remains after one has forgotten what one has learned in school.

Albert Einstein
physicist

Learning Objectives

1. Provide the patient advocate supporting educational materials for working with individuals.
2. Introduce techniques for individuals to take control of their health information.
3. Learn to recognize potential roadblocks in managing your healthcare.
4. Understand the healthcare perspective among different stakeholders.

Overview

The key issue with patient health information is the lack of a health data-centric portal. This results from the current inability among all stakeholders to transfer and aggregate an individual health data report, similar to a credit report within the financial industry. The Personal Health Portfolio (PHP) model is a patient-centric health data management model. In Section III of this book, the portfolio describes the critical data elements contained within standardized topic frameworks of how those data elements relate to each other. The frameworks are segmented into "health," "wellness management," "financial," and "personal health assessments." This model is an illustration in practice of creating, managing, validating, and updating patient-centric health information in a meaningful way to facilitate an individual's defined health objectives. The model has the following strategic objectives:

■ Aggregate critical data points that will increase an individual's ability to
  – Make the best informed healthcare decision
  – Manage healthcare costs
  – Manage ongoing health
  – Avoid adverse health events
  – Avoid adverse financial events
  – Select the right resources at the right time
  – Build self-confidence
  – Self-advocate in a meaningful, productive way

Taking Control

Congratulations on your decision to read this book. As a patient advocator, helping people take control is the first step for empowerment. This starts with helping people become reacquainted with topics such as

■ How to ask the right question
■ How to find the right resource
■ How to stay healthy
■ How to manage the pace of technology

As individuals enter the healthcare system, they can become captive to a mind-numbing maze of rules, regulations, arcane coding systems, privacy issues, and so on. All of it makes obtaining the right care with minimum risk and cost a difficult challenge. This book will help advocates guide the right decision-making for others as well as assist individuals themselves in regaining control of their health or that of a loved one. Also included in this book are instructions to complete a PHP.

The goal is to help patients become their own best advocates for their physical and mental well-being and to learn when to get help from a trained patient advocate.

The PHP process described in this book is the product of many years of experience, research, and proven results in resolving patient issues. It is designed to help people avoid making bad medical and financial decisions about their health. It does not matter who makes a bad decision (whether it's the doctor, insurance company, or anybody else involved in the patient's care), but the result of one can be physically and financially disastrous for the patient and their family.

Important: In today's complex world of healthcare, information is power. People who do not have all of the facts necessary to navigate the healthcare system are almost certain to make decisions that result in more problems that affect the availability and quality of care they receive (and the financial implications).

The PHP is designed to help the individual gather all the facts necessary to make a good decision about their health. One particularly important benefit of a PHP is its guidance on organizing and protecting what is known as Protected Health Information (PHI). PHI is data pertaining to the medical history and ongoing care of a patient. It is protected by a statute, which means it can only be known to the patient and their medical caregivers, unless the patient provides specific permission for third party access.

With PHI under the firm control of the patient, decisions can result in the best possible outcome—that is, "the best treatment option at the most reasonable cost."

Patient Message: Take charge of your information by getting it into your own hands and controlling it.

Guiding Patients in Managing Their Health

A PHP works much like a resume. A resume is designed to describe to a prospective employer who you are, where you have been, and what you have done over the course of your career. Similarly, a patient's PHP illustrates who they are, where they have been, and what they have done to manage their health. Patients can choose to share their PHPs with the people who are involved in their care. This could include a doctor, a loved one, or anybody else who is critical to the patient's well-being. The patient can choose to keep their PHP as private as they would like, and may decide to only share specific portions of their PHP on a need-to-know basis.

Patient Instruction Example

When you go to a bank to apply for a loan, the bank reviews your credit report to assess your credit risk—that is, it determines how likely it is that you will be able to pay off the loan. It uses this risk assessment to determine the best loan options for you. Similarly, a PHP helps you and your doctors determine your current level of health risk and what the best treatment options are for you, based on that risk assessment.

The only difference is that while banks can readily access a complete credit history, doctors *cannot* easily assemble a complete picture of a patient's health history. This is because you have most likely seen a multitude of doctors and been treated at different hospitals and clinics over the course of your lifetime.

Doctors, therefore, do not have direct access to all of your health history from a single source. Most or all of the pieces of your health history can be found with the different doctors and facilities that have been involved in your care. Unfortunately, we are still many years away from having a centralized database that is able to share a person's complete healthcare history in the same way as credit reporting agencies can. As with the financial industry, many standards on privacy and access must be established in order to ensure that such a centralized organization protects the privacy of your information.

Until then, use your PHP so that your doctors have access to all the personal health details they need to deliver the best possible care.

Patient Message: Managing your health requires organizing your information.

Getting Good Care

Unfortunately, the healthcare market is fragmented. The best defense is a good offense. In a fragmented market, the patient must be organized and armed with their own information. The patient advocate should include a discussion on how organizing all of the patient's data impacts the quality of care.

Patient Instruction Example

When you visit a new doctor, hospital, or pharmacy, you should ask to review your entire health history. However, this rarely happens. One reason is time constraints. Another reason is that staff do not have access to your entire health history from other providers. Armed with your PHP, you can provide them with your complete health history. (Conversely, if a new doctor or other provider lacks a complete picture of your history, you are asking them to give you treatment without knowing everything about you.)

With an accurate and up-to-date PHP, you can communicate with your doctors, nurses, and pharmacists. This greatly enhances your chances of

- Staying healthy
- Experiencing less stress and anxiety
- Correctly following up on instructions for your treatment

Problem: Many patients do not understand what their doctors tell them. Many are confused about their treatment instructions. Poor communication can lead to misdiagnosed illnesses, unnecessary tests, and a failure to follow instructions properly.

Do not blame your doctors or professional staff for miscommunication, or the lack thereof. The healthcare system is under stressful time constraints. Make it your job to prepare questions ahead of time. Make sure that your questions are fully answered. Make it your job to understand these answers before you leave your appointment. Keep your questions brief, and if you are interrupted, return to your question until it is answered.[1] Remember, there is no such thing as a dumb question when it comes to your health.

Patient Message: The next phase in managing your PHP is actually advocating for yourself while you are engaged within the healthcare system. This could simply involve asking questions about the medical issue at hand. Though this may sound obvious or even trivial, it is especially necessary when your gut tells you, "Hey, this just does not sound right."

Case Example

The case of Kerry Higuera, a mother of four who lives in Peoria, Arizona, is an unfortunate example of this. Kerry was pregnant and in her first trimester. She started to bleed and was worried that she might be having a miscarriage. Kerry went to the emergency room for an evaluation. Kerry explained her experience to CNN (television program) as follows:

> "The nurse said, 'Kerry?' and I said, 'Yes,' and she said, "I"m going to take you for a little walk' and I followed her down the hallway."

> "She brought me to the CT scan room, and I asked, 'Is this really what I need to have done?' And the nurse said, 'Yes, this is what the doctor wants. He wants a CT scan of your abdomen,' and I said, 'OK.' After the scan, the nurse led me back to a room to wait for the doctor."

> "I was so scared. I told my husband, I'm sure I've had a miscarriage. I'm sure the doctor is going to come and tell us we lost the baby."[2]

Kerry Higuera did not need a C.T. scan! The misidentification of the patient initiated a series of one bad event after another. The hospital administrator, doctor, and radiologist came in to explain that an error had occurred. Another patient with the name Kerry was supposed to receive the CT scan for abdominal pain and staff had confused Kerry with this other patient. After delivery, Kerry's baby began to suffer severe cognitive issues (brain damage). The injury was likely caused when the fetus was exposed to the radiation from the CT scan.

Lesson Learned: Be firm. If something does not make sense, be diligent in your questions. Had Kerry been more aggressive with her instincts about the CT scan, her baby would have been born healthy and without complications.

Patient Message: Getting good care is dependent on having complete and accurate medical information.

Managing the Fast Pace of Technology

Healthcare providers are developing new tools to help manage their patients. At the same time, entrepreneurs are exploding with offerings in the market to provide patients with technology tools, which range from managing finances and health records to having confidence in making the right decision for patients' healthcare needs. As with any new tool, do your homework. Check references and really understand who is providing the service and how it is being provided.

Common buzz words among healthcare professionals include "data consolidation," "mobile health," "interoperability to communicate, exchange, and share health information," "best-of-breed healthcare ecosystem," and "healthcare cloud." Other technology tools include 3-D printing and predictive and prescriptive analytics. With the exception of 3-D printing, the trends are data-related, thus emphasizing the need for every healthcare consumer to develop their own data-tracking systems. Do not be intimidated by all the buzz words and introductions of new approaches.

Patient Advocate Consideration: It Is *Always* about People

Managing the Generational Healthcare Gap

Managing health is about people and their data. All of us must take personal responsibility for managing personal health information, or we risk becoming susceptible to nefarious entities trying to steal our identities.

Reality of Overall Healthcare: A Market in Transition

Healthcare is on the radar of each and every individual from a multitude of perspectives. First are the differences between the private (employer insurance) and public sector (government-sponsored insurance). Next, you have patients, providers of care, those that pay healthcare claims, and of course, organizations that provide benefit coverage. Then, you have both federal and state legislatures passing various rules, laws, and programs. The Affordable Care Act and subsequent modifications continue to impact individuals and those who work within the industry. Technology is hitting the market from all fronts. With any new, rapid change, growing pains will manifest themselves in different formats. New technology systems may become vulnerable from a security perspective. Investment is needed to train personnel in using the new technology. The list can be exhaustive, so at a minimum, patients just have an awareness. In the meantime, patients can take control of their own information, and update and manage it. At this point, it is not so much the technology that an individual uses but the accumulation and access to their information as it is created that is critical. Why?

- Example: Aunt Susan was taken to the hospital for her elective surgery at 6:30 a.m. Upon arrival, her nephew noted that the hospital staff were struggling and upset. After some time had passed, the registration clerk confessed that Aunt Susan's entire electronic medical record had disappeared. Fortunately, her nephew had a hard copy of her entire file with him.

Lesson Learned: Do not wait any further—take control of your information in the format that is most comfortable, be it electronic and/or good old-fashioned paper.

Reality of Healthcare for Patients: The Plague of Medical Identity Theft

Another risk facing patients as a by-product of the complexity of our healthcare system is the creation of vulnerabilities among patients who are exploited by criminals in regard to issues such as identity theft and fraud.

Identity theft is the crime of stealing someone's so-called Personally Identifiable Information (PII). Such information includes your social security number, driver's license number, credit card data, birth date, telephone number, health insurance identification, employment identification information, and so on.

Typically, identity theft is the precursor to identity *fraud*. Such fraud includes making unauthorized purchases with stolen credit card information, using stolen social security numbers to obtain fraudulent identification such as a driver's license, opening bank accounts in the identity theft victim's name, obtaining medical care under the victim's name, and so on.

EXAMPLE 1

Jim and Carrie (not their actual names) received a collection notice from a clinic. The notice said that they owed $104.00 for the treatment of their 3-week-old son, Scott. Oddly, the notice that Jim and Carrie received included Scott's middle name. Nobody knew Scott's middle name except for close family members and the hospital where the paperwork was filed to get his social security number. Carrie instantly became suspicious of the collection notice. She could not remember whether Scott had received the medical services listed in the notice. Then, new bills for medical services started arriving in the mail. These bills were for medical services not performed on her son and were from doctors' offices located in other states. Jim and Carrie knew something was wrong. After numerous phone calls, they learned that Scott's identity and health information had been stolen when they applied for the social security card through the hospital. The clinic had not properly protected Scott's PII. A group of dishonest individuals stole and sold his information to receive free healthcare services under Scott's name on Jim and Carrie's dime.[3]

Sometimes, you can become the victim of poor or improper care due to simple errors that occur on a frequent basis throughout the healthcare system. The good news is that if you're proactive about your and your family's healthcare, the serious consequences of these errors can be avoided.

EXAMPLE 2

Annie (not her real name) is a mother of four children. Her last child had been born more than 5 years ago. She was visited by a state social worker at her home. The social worker wanted to take away her children. Annie was rightly scared and confused. She was a very good mother and cared very well for her children.

Annie's problem began when she lost her wallet that contained her insurance card, which was found by a drug user by the name of Christine. When Christine gave birth at a local hospital, she used Annie's identification. Christine's baby had tested positive for illegal drugs. The social worker wanted to take away Annie's children because they thought that Annie had delivered a baby with drugs in her bloodstream. Fortunately, Annie was able to keep her children.

However, Annie's problems were not over. Months later, Annie went to a different local hospital for treatment of a kidney infection. When Christine had her baby, her medical records had been mixed into Annie's file. Fortunately, since Annie had become more careful about her health information, she corrected the blood type listed in her doctor's file before her procedure.

Lesson Learned: Without attention to detail, Annie might have died and her children might have ended up in social services.[3] In addition, had Annie maintained an up-to-date PHP (before her wallet was stolen), it may have helped her dig herself out of the identity fraud quagmire that victimized her.

Patient Instruction Example: Risk

As some of the previous examples indicate, a PHP is not a silver bullet for preventing errors in healthcare but can certainly help avoid them or minimize the damage by early detection of the problem. Errors beyond your control can still happen and, like Annie, only attention to detail can protect you. In Kerry's case, had she been more aggressive about asking questions and getting the answers she needed, her baby might not have suffered the brain damage that was caused by the hospital's mistake.

However, in most instances, a PHP will help protect your personal medical information from fraud, waste, and abuse. The healthcare industry grows larger every year. Willie Sutton, a famous bank robber, was once asked, "Why do you rob banks?" His response was simple but clever: "Because that's where the money is." There is a lot of money in healthcare, and everyone wants a piece of it.

We live in a buyer-beware world. This means that you must be responsible for and remain in control of your healthcare information. You need to be the guardian of your healthcare information to make sure that no one uses it inappropriately.

Patient Message: The reality of healthcare is that mistakes happen and dishonest opportunists will allow greed to take over, even at the expense of others.

Patient Advocate Consideration: Recap on Other Forms of "Identity" Under Threat

Traditional identity theft is the intent to use another individual's identity (outside of healthcare) to commit, aid, or abet any unlawful activity. What does it look like? Opening up a credit card and going shopping on another person's credit.

Synthetic identity theft is the intent to use another individual's identity via the creation of fake/stolen information to make a hybrid identity to commit, aid, or abet any unlawful activity. What does it look like? Someone takes a real name and associates that person with a fake business. That person may fabricate income to get credit.

Professional identity theft is the intent to use another's professional identity to commit, aid, or abet any unlawful activity. What does this look like? A person may steal a nurse's license number, take on her identity as a nurse, and get a job in a hospital. A doctor was arrested in Florida because he opened up a clinic, was treating patients, and was getting paid under the license of a deceased doctor.

Reality of Healthcare for Providers

Healthcare providers are faced with difficult challenges in accepting numerous types of insurance, including Medicare, Medicaid, private insurance contracts, and patients with no insurance. The contracts can be completely different from one party to another. For example, one of the biggest misconceptions about Medicare and hospitals is that Medicare does not pay on the itemized charges that providers document on their bills. They pay on a completely different system called DRGs (diagnosis-related groups). This means that, instead of paying for a list of itemized charges, the hospital is paid based on the patient's diagnosis. It is a flat fee system in which the payments for diagnosis groups are predetermined.

An individual does not need to understand all of the different ways that healthcare is paid. It is important just to understand that many different formulas exist. The following is an example of healthcare from the providers' point of view.

A patient has a heart attack. The incident must be treated the same way, regardless of who is paying the bill, whether it's the patient's employer, the employer's insurance company, or a third-party administrator (TPA). Unfortunately, some contracts create conflicting incentives from one payer contract (a payer contract is the benefit/insurance plan that is purchased by the employer for health benefits) to another. As a patient, be aware that a different rule may govern how your healthcare services are being paid. The questions to ask is "What am I being charged, and how is my service being billed?" As for healthcare providers, some of their headaches are illustrated by the following personal real-life examples:

- ■ **"Getting bills paid and working with patients is a time-consuming task."** This is the perspective from an orthopedic practice in Chicago. The business office manager provided a sample of the practice's most difficult healthcare claims to collect payment on.

  The follow-up for one patient's claim took more than an hour.

  (Please note that, at this time, the claim was nearly a year old and the staff had already spent over 30 hours attempting to collect payment.)

  These are the highlights in working with the insurer: "Hello, concerning claim number 123456, can you tell me why this claim is being denied?" The claims adjustor reported, "The CPT (Current Procedural Terminology) code the doctor selected is experimental." The office staff responded, "Really? This procedure has been around for over 20 years and is routinely performed. Can you tell me where on your web site you report this procedure as experimental?" She responded, "We don't have any lists on our web site." The next question: "Is it in the employer's benefit plan document that this is a service you do not cover?" She followed up, "No." Further, "Is it documented or communicated to the patient anywhere that this is a service that you do not cover?" She stated, "No, we don't list all of the services we do not cover."

  She followed up, "However, if the doctor would bill the service with this CPT code, we will pay for it." The CPT code suggested to be used instead does not reflect the service provided. In addition, it would reduce the payment by 20%. The office staff simply followed up with, "Are you suggesting that the doctor submits a false claim?"

  The story becomes more interesting. The office staff called the hospital where the patient received the services and asked if they had received payment for this patient's bill. The hospital reported that they had indeed been paid—within 30 days of submitting their bill. The office staff called the claims adjustor back. The question presented to her: "Why is it experimental for the doctor to do this surgery and not get paid, but OK for the hospital to let the doctor do the surgery and receive payment for the experimental procedure?" The call was placed on hold. After a 10 minute wait, the claims adjustor came back and said that the doctor was just using the wrong code.

Lesson Learned: This is an example of what a business office within a physician setting experiences on a daily basis. In the meantime, the patient is "stuck" in the middle, wondering why the doctor never informed her that the procedure was experimental.

- **A complex reimbursement system: Learning to follow the money in healthcare.** This example is from a hospital's business office, specifically, from the office's collection staff. They were having difficulty with a claim and the family was very upset. The claim involved a very sick child with a seven-figure hospital bill. The family's insurance company had a contract with the hospital providing for a 20% discount on hospital charges. The plan also had a $5000 annual deductible per family. Here is the math:

$1,000,000 total hospital bill
$800,000 total with the 20% insurance contract discount applied
$5,000 deductible to be paid by the family
$795,000 to be paid by the insurance plan

The hospital received a $400,000 payment, leaving a balance of $395,000. That receivable was sent to collection. The hospital then contacted the family to pay the remaining balance of the bill. The payer (insurance company) stated that it had paid only $400,000 because the patient's family had hit its lifetime benefit cap of $1 million. (The payer had applied the hospitals original amount billed of $1 million toward the lifetime cap; in addition, on all prior bills the payer had applied the original amount billed by the provider, which was $600,000 in charges—not the amount they had paid.) As a result, the patient's family had quickly hit the $1 million threshold. The math is confusing, because what was being applied was the amount billed and NOT what was paid.

Question: How are the hospital and the collector going to solve this problem? A follow-up call was initiated with the claims adjustor from the insurance company, with the question: "It appears that the patient has met the lifetime cap of $1,000,000. Is that correct?" The adjustor responded, "Yes—that is why we sent a payment of $400,000. The patient will be responsible for the rest."

When a patient gets hit with one large bill, it is easy to see the adverse dynamics of what happens from time to time. The patient had a $1 million bill. The payer applied the total amount of this bill toward the lifetime cap. They applied the hospital's original billed amount, regardless of what they actually paid out. What they did not do was apply the discounted amount of $800,000, or the $795,000 that was to be paid toward the lifetime cap. This is just one small, misunderstood dynamic of how following the numbers can drive all market players crazy in healthcare, including the patient, the provider, and the plan sponsor (who is most likely to be the recipient of complaints from very upset families). **(If you are confused, that is OK—it's a numbers game.)**

A subsequent follow-up occurred with the claims adjustor. "Would you like us to explain to the parents of this sick child that what you are doing is applying the total original charges to their lifetime cap?" Silence on the phone. Further, "Would you like us to explain that they have to pay $395,000 out of pocket because you want to take credit for the original charges of the hospital and not the amount that you actually paid?" Keep in mind that premiums are based on the patient's risk. This leaves a very complex, unanswered question in the market. Are premiums for insurance based on what hospitals bill out or on what they actually get paid? This information is not transparent and is considered proprietary (a company trade secret).

Patient Message: Providers have too many contracts to manage among all their private and public payers. The number of provider employees (e.g., surgeons and nurses) requiring payment on one claim has increased over the years. As a patient, you can benefit from understanding this and learning to be firm and persistent when asking who is involved with making decisions about how claims are handled.

Note: This event occurred prior to the Affordable Care Act. In the current environment, the concept of a lifetime cap was removed, in addition to penalties resulting from a preexisting condition. However, the arbitrage that occurs with monies between parties is still not transparent.

Reality of Healthcare for Payers

Healthcare is a $3 trillion and growing marketplace, as measured by the Centers for Medicare and Medicaid Services (CMS).* Keep in mind that $1 trillion in $1 bills would weigh about 1.1 million tons. A Nimitz-class aircraft carrier weighs about 97,000 tons. Therefore, $1 trillion in $1 bills would weigh more than 11 aircraft carriers.† Healthcare would require at least 22 aircraft carriers to accommodate the dollars our market moves. In addition, the "paper" required would be about $26,400,000 in trees for each trillion dollars processed.

Some additional perspectives on these numbers:

■ $6,027,397,260.27 spent per day
■ $251,141,552.51 per hour
■ $4,185,692.54 per minute

* http://www.cms.hhs.gov/NationalHealthExpendData/downloads/highlights.pdf
† http://bitsofbrain.wordpress.com/2009/06/30/how-much-is-a-trillion-dollars/

When you combine the volume of claims processed by private payer systems and TPAs for our government programs, the amount of money being lost to fraud, waste, and abuse is estimated at about $400,000 per minute. That is $210.2 *billion* per year.

Do the math: According to the Association of Certified Fraud Examiners,* 7%, or $990 billion, of revenue in the United States is lost to fraud. Roughly one-fifth of total fraud losses in the United States is due to healthcare fraud (plus waste and abuse, if there is a real difference).

That is not pocket change. That is a lot of money to spread among a lot of crooks. And make no mistake—the crooks in the U.S. healthcare system are not just career con artists who go around making a living out of scamming the system. They are also dishonest medical doctors, pharmacists, pharmacy companies, medical equipment manufacturers, payers, TPAs, patients, employers, and others.

Claims adjustors—the professionals who review the submitted claims—have their work cut out for them. One of the reasons these people are on guard can be explained by reviewing the following actual cases:

- "Dozens arrested in healthcare fraud scheme; Doctors among those accused in scam to bill Medicare through false claims."[†] In this case, about $371 million in false Medicare claims were identified and about 145 people across the country were charged.
- "32 accused of $60 million of Medicare fraud in three states."[‡] The 32 indicted suspects specialized in creating fake patients and would bill Medicare for unnecessary medical equipment, physical therapy, and HIV infusions.
- A survey conducted from 2000 to 2007 found payments for medical services ordered by over 16,500 deceased doctors totaling between $60 million and $92 million. Some doctors had been dead for more than 10 years.[§]
- Rent-a-patient schemes involve planting employees within an organization to act as recruiters for dishonest providers by offering health insurance to vulnerable "coworkers." They pay these employees to receive medically unnecessary services. The company (or its insurance company) pays the crooked provider on the bogus claims submitted for these unnecessary or often nonexistent services. I have had several employers who have had seven-figure losses due to the rent-a-patient scheme.[¶]

---

* www.acfe.com
[†] http://www.msnbc.msn.com/id/32205408/
[‡] http://news.yahoo.com/s/ap/20091215/ap_on_bi_ge/us_medicare_fraud_busts
[§] Senate Permanent Subcommittee on Investigations Press Release, "Coleman, Levin Investigate Millions in Medicare Payments for Claims Tied to Deceased Doctors," July 8, 2008.
[¶] "Bodies for Rent" John Wiley & Sons.

These examples represent a small sample of the schemes that are constantly being perpetrated throughout today's healthcare marketplace. This is one of the reasons why payers have created some of the barriers that we see today.

Patient Message: Payers receive numerous requests for payments for legitimate and illegitimate services. Make sure that you understand your rights according to your insurance plan document. Be vigilant that no one has stolen your identity to shop for healthcare services.

Reality of Healthcare for Employers

Nongovernment employers cover about 50% of total healthcare expenditures. However, costs are increasing and employers are looking for new savings opportunities. They want employees to participate in wellness programs and become conscientious consumers as they select and make their health choices.

In addition, there are numerous government and private sector initiatives to use new technology to improve the delivery of care and reduce the costs associated with providing it.

Employers can make costly "wrong turns" in the healthcare maze, just as individual patients can. Some of these mistakes are unavoidable because the market is resolving how we deliver healthcare, the dynamics of access, and other legislated attributes that are shifting. However, one area in which employers do have control is education.

Unfortunately, as pointed out in one authoritative book on the subject, "Patient education is often invisible in management's eyes because it is frequently undocumented, unmonitored and underappreciated for the skill and experience it demands. The positive impact of effective patient education on health outcomes and costs is not taken into account in day-to-day healthcare delivery."[4]

Employers who invest in educating their employees on how to advocate for themselves when making healthcare decisions can realize substantial savings in their healthcare expenses. Though this is easier said than done, it is hoped that this book will serve as a useful educational tool for employers who choose this approach to save on the costs of healthcare.

Also Important: Employers must educate *themselves* about what exactly they are paying for. However, again, this is not as simple as it could be.
Key challenges for employers:

■ **Employer profile #1:** This company is an overseas-based employer. It is self-insured in the United States and pays $40 million per year for its group healthcare claims within the United States. The company has employees in almost every state.
We initiated an audit of the funds being taken from the company's account by their TPA every 2 weeks. An audit could not be initiated without a specific auditor contract with the TPA, outlining exactly what could and could not be audited.

Result: The company had no idea what it was paying for in the way of specific healthcare services. It therefore had no way of knowing if it was paying too much, whether it was being defrauded, or whether it was complying with all U.S. employment laws and regulations. How could management educate employees on cost-saving healthcare decisions without any of this critical information?

■ **Employer profile #2:** This is a small firm, with most of its employees located in one state. The company pays $3 million per year in healthcare claims. An audit agreement with the payer stipulated that recoveries were to be limited. The $3 million per year represented 15,000 claims; however, their TPA would not allow them to audit more than 250 claims. **That means this employer and the employees who were paid out of pocket contractually were not allowed to verify more than 250 of the claims.**

■ **Employer profile #3:** This large, publicly traded company was told by its TPA that it had no right to audit its self-insured employer benefit plan. Despite its $100 million annual payout in healthcare claims, this company too was operating completely in the dark regarding the breakdown of its payouts, the appropriateness of services rendered to employees, the existence or absence of fraud, and so on.

Other restrictions experienced by employers and others include
  – Audit limitation of no more than 250 claims.
  – No audit allowance at all.
  – No provision for paying the audit vendor on contingency.
  – Restrictions on contacting providers due to "proprietary relationships."
  – Complete audit independence. The payer has the right to review and make changes to the auditor's report prior to providing it to the employer.
  – Fees to third parties that are not listed on payer invoices.
  – Pharmaceutical claims that do not belong to them but that must be paid because of pharmacy error.
  – Employer auditors being prohibited from auditing psychiatric claims, including treatment for depression and substance abuse, because they are "too confidential."
  – Claims files provided for auditing not having the listing of who received the payer's check and/or not having the license number of the provider.
  – Claim files provided for auditing containing only partial details and data on claims.
  – Recovery audits being prohibited.

Patient Message: As an employee, your premiums are being impacted by these contracts, in addition to your employers' ability to hire and/or provide additional compensation. In the long run, we all pay for this. In this book, the background information is presented to allow a better understanding of everything that is happening in the healthcare marketplace.

Inequities exist in the overall healthcare market when not all of the stakeholders are subject to the same set of conditions. In order for the U.S. healthcare system to function effectively, the rules must be the same for all parties and different types of market players. If hospitals are subjected to contingency-based audits from government-sponsored healthcare programs as well as from the private payers' programs, then payers should be subject to the same audit rights by employers. In other words, many payers do not allow their customer (the private employer) to audit all associated monetary transactions.

However, the provider is subject to audits by both private and government payers. This creates an imbalance or unfair leverage by private payers over providers. In addition, private employers are vulnerable to not fully understanding what they are paying for. By the same token, patients should have a right to information so they can understand their healthcare plans. Similarly, payers should have the right to investigate the legitimacy of claims they are required to pay, while providers should be fairly compensated for medically necessary care.

Let's add another layer of craziness. Are you ready? How do you know who has the authority to resolve disputes? The rules change depending on who is involved and how the health plan originated. Here are some real-life scenarios:

- An individual/employee can have health insurance, which means the state department of insurance is their boss. Any appeals can be submitted to the state and be taken to court. The claims are paid by a vendor insurance company.
- For an employee who has insurance with a self-insured employer, their boss is the Employee Retirement Income Security Act (ERISA). They can appeal to the plan, be protected by ERISA, and be taken to court for disputes. The claims are then paid by a vendor TPA (who also can be an insurance company).
- A federal employee can have health benefits that are managed through the Office of Personnel Management (OPM). Any disputes cannot be taken to court, and ERISA does not protect them (claims are paid by a TPA).
- A state employee can have health benefits through a self-insured program in which, in essence, the plan itself is the boss. Any disputes cannot be taken to court, and ERISA does not protect (claims are paid by a TPA).
- In the following scenario, a patient goes to a hospital, receives services, and the bill is sent to a medical review company hired by a TPA/insurance company. The review company gets paid on contingency—a potential audit conflict of interest. They deny a portion of a hospital bill, alleging that the service was experimental. The individual with insurance can appeal to the plan and the state and litigate while the hospital pursues them for the balance. The ERISA employee can appeal to the plan and litigate while the hospital pursues them for the balance. The federal employee can appeal to the Office of Personal Management (OPM), not litigate, and still be pursued by the hospital for the balance. The state employee can appeal to the plan, not litigate, and still be pursued by the hospital for the balance (too much to even include Medicare/Medicaid).

Patient Message: Employers cannot make sound business decisions without access to complete and accurate information. You should only enter into agreements that have right to audit provisions with no limitation on validating expenditures of the plan. Once you have a full picture of your healthcare expenditures, use that information to educate your employees on how to self-advocate and avoid being a victim of a confusing and fragmented system.

Overview of the Healthcare Problem

The prior sections provided examples of specific issues among key stakeholders: the patient, the provider, the payer, and the employer. This is an overview of the top categories affecting all stakeholders. They include the complexity of identity theft, which is the fastest growing area of organized crime and has become a complicated business. The next growing problem is the ongoing submission of false claims, which simply means third parties submitting claims for healthcare services not provided or needed. As a result, teaching patients how to review their medical health information is just as important as supporting their ongoing healthcare needs. Subsequent chapters will provide material on the information to request from healthcare providers, health benefit programs and or insurance companies. The material will also explain what to look for to make sure that no one is submitting false claims for medical services, prescriptions, supplies and or medical equipment under your identity.

Another growing problem that is not generally understood by most is the corporate misconduct among healthcare organizations. That could range from organized misrepresentation of services to the pricing of services. Finally, a significant area of concern involves the vulnerable population and general healthcare management issues.

Theft and Inappropriate Use of an Identity

An identity includes a person's name, age, date of birth, and other identifiers, such as social security number. When a third party uses your identity, it is considered identity theft. When your identity is used within the healthcare system, it is considered medical identity theft, as noted in an earlier example.

When a third party uses the license of a professional to provide services, it is considered professional identity theft. What does that look like? An individual assuming the name and license of a doctor sets up a clinic and treats patients as if they were licensed. Any service provided by an unlicensed individual is considered a false claim. Legitimate claims must be provided by licensed professionals.

Note: Most states have the ability to look up the license of a professional. Make sure the license is active and that the address of the provider is matching the address provided by your doctor.

Once your identity is misused in healthcare, keep in mind that other medical records are now being mingled with your real records. In essence, you now have a synthetic identity. That means a new hybrid identity has evolved, and your records need to be cleaned up. A patient advocate would be a great resource to start the process of cleaning up false records created in your name.

Misrepresentation of Claims for Services Provided

The following is a list of the classic types of misrepresentation that can occur with healthcare bills and services. Patient advocates are in a prime position to educate on what to look for and how to look at it when it comes to patients' medical record, requests for details of their bills, and finally how to "audit" their own information. The following list includes examples of misrepresentation that a patient advocate should include in his or her instruction materials when working with individuals. Teach them how to look for red flags.

- Billing for services not rendered (look at the bill—do you see anything that you do not recall discussing with your doctor?).
- Billing for a noncovered service as a covered service (documenting in your record a different service than what was done so your insurance company will pay for it).
- Misrepresenting dates of service (changing the date of service from the real one so it will get paid).
- Misrepresenting locations of service (stating that the service was done in an outpatient setting vs. a clinic so the provider will get more money).
- Misrepresenting providers of service (billing for a doctor when it was the assistant who provided the service, so a higher rate is paid).
- Incorrect reporting of diagnoses or procedures (includes unbundling) (listing a diagnosis for a condition that you don't have to make it easier for your bill to get paid).
- Overutilization of services (providing more services than what you medically need).
- Corruption (kickbacks and bribery) (bribing you to get services you do not need).
- False or unnecessary issuance of prescription drugs (prescribing medications that you don't need).

Corporate Misconduct

The best way to understand corporate misconduct is to look at cases in which parties have been investigated, fined, or not allowed to participate as healthcare providers. In essence, the corporation adopts practices that result in unjustified payments or outright fraud.

■ **Example of services billed but not rendered**
- Nevada: An x-ray technician provided items and services to Quality Medical Imaging (QMI) patients that were billed to federal healthcare programs. QMI, Nevada, entered into a $34,187.34 settlement agreement with the Office of Inspector General (OIG).

■ **Examples of services provided by individuals whose licenses were excluded**
- California: Bills were submitted for vaccinations by a professional who was excluded from participation. Quest Diagnostics Incorporated (Quest), Summit Health, Inc. (Summit), and Unilab Corporation (Unilab) entered into a $126,599.25 settlement agreement with the OIG.
- Wisconsin: The Home Health Agency agreed to voluntary exclude themselves from participation in the Wisconsin Medicaid program for submitting bills for services not rendered.
- Illinois: The Illinois Hospital Corporation settled a case involving excluded individuals. The Advocate Health and Hospitals Corporation (Advocate) in Illinois entered into a $317,660.89 settlement agreement with the OIG. The settlement agreement resolved allegations that Advocate had employed individuals who were excluded from participation in any federal healthcare program.

■ **Examples of pricing irregularities**
- Glenmark Pharmaceuticals, Inc. USA (Glenmark), New Jersey, entered into a $2,887,300 settlement agreement with the OIG. The settlement resolved allegations that Glenmark failed to timely submit monthly and quarterly average manufacturer's price (AMP) data to the CMS for certain months and quarters. The Medicaid Drug Rebate Program requires pharmaceutical companies to enter into and have in effect a national rebate agreement with the Secretary of Health and Human Services in order for Medicaid payments to be available for the pharmaceutical company's covered drugs. Companies with such rebate agreements are required to submit certain drug pricing information to the CMS, including quarterly and monthly AMP data. Senior Counsel Nicole Caucci represented the OIG.
- Ascend Laboratories, LLC (Ascend), New Jersey, entered into a $1,287,000 settlement agreement with the OIG. The settlement agreement resolved allegations that Ascend failed to submit monthly and quarterly AMP data to the CMS for certain months and quarters. The Medicaid Drug Rebate Program requires pharmaceutical companies to enter into and have in effect a national rebate agreement with the Secretary of Health and Human Services in order for Medicaid payments to be available for the pharmaceutical company's covered drugs. Companies with such rebate agreements are required to submit certain drug pricing information to the CMS, including quarterly and monthly AMP data.

Vulnerable Population

The vulnerable population is an ongoing concern. These are pockets of individuals who may be compromised because of their age. Age includes both youth and elders. Another vulnerable group are those who have physical and/or cognitive disabilities. The following is a listing of three critical areas:

■ Medicaid children are often targeted and exposed to unnecessary treatments. The Small Smiles Dental Centers illustrate an example of this exploitation:
  – Over 300,000 children treated improperly.
  – The defendants conspired to perform unnecessary procedures and use unnecessary physical restraints upon children in order to fraudulently obtain extra compensation.
  – Medicaid-eligible children had appointments for routine check-ups and cleaning at the defendants' clinics. They would be given x-rays, a cleaning, and then the dentist would evaluate the child's mouth.
  – The x-rays were often unnecessary and taken incorrectly by employees not licensed to operate the x-ray machine, and were sometimes unreadable or even blank.
  – Parents/guardians were then brought to a consultation room where they were told that their child needed extensive work, including root canals and steel crowns.
  – Parents were pressured to sign consent forms immediately so that the extensive procedures could be done on the same day as the initial consultation. The defendants thought that if the patients left the building, they might obtain a second opinion about the need for additional procedures and might not return.

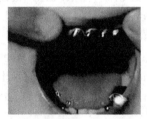

  – This is an example of unnecessary and inappropriate treatment: the placing of steel caps on baby teeth.
■ Elder abuse, exploitation, and neglect are also targets. Elders are targeted by strangers, known parties, and even family. Examples of this include
  – Seniors being targeted for overpricing, fake claims, and mismanaged care
  – Being exposed to substandard care
  – Experiencing an adverse event, which affects one in seven
■ Another vulnerable population are individuals with intellectual and physical disabilities.* The type of challenges this group experiences includes:

---

* http://disability-abuse.com/survey/survey-report.pdf

– A study reporting that people with disabilities who were victims reported having experienced various types of abuse.
  • Some 87.2% reported verbal-emotional abuse, 50.6% physical abuse, 41.6% sexual abuse, 37.3% neglect, and 31.5% financial abuse.

Key General Health Management Issues: Three Critical Areas

The following is a list of three critical areas impacting the cost and delivery of healthcare services.

■ **Excessive dispensing of narcotics** and pain killers in the general population
  – Doctors who are the most prolific prescribers of powerful narcotic pain-killers and stimulants often have worrisome records, a ProPublica analysis of Medicare data shows.*
■ **Misrepresenting disability** claims statuses, workers' compensation, and other benefit programs
  – "NY charges 106 individuals in huge fraud over disability claims."†
■ Ineffective management of **behavioral health issues**
  – Mental illness and psychiatric support
  – Support of youth re-entry from the criminal system

Patient Message: The healthcare "problem" is deeply rooted in antiquated practices, systems, and engrained culture that have contributed to the current state. Simple notions such as customer service are just starting to take form. The level of dysfunction is presented only for awareness. The best solution for the individual patient is to collect their information, manage it, understand it and have it readily accessible.

Study Questions

1. What does PHP stand for?
   a. Personal Healthcare Protocol
   b. Personal Healthcare Presentation
   c. Personal Healthcare Proof
   d. Personal Healthcare Portfolio
2. What is a key challenge in managing your healthcare?
   a. Obtaining the right care with minimum risk and cost
   b. Getting good care, no matter what the cost or risk is

---

* http://www.usatoday.com/story/news/nation/2014/12/15/doctors-prescription-painkillers/20428639/
† http://www.nytimes.com/2014/01/08/nyregion/retired-new-york-officers-and-firefighters-charged-in-social-security-scheme.html

   c. Protecting your identity
   d. Helping you avoid bad medical and financial decisions
3. What role can a patient advocate support?
   a. Help you to become your own best advocate for your physical and mental well-being
   b. Advise when to get help from supplemental resources
   c. Both A and B
   d. None of the above
4. What is a PHP?
   a. A self-compiled collection of all information related to your health and healthcare history
   b. Your healthcare diary
   c. Your PHP is designed to help you gather all the facts necessary to make good decisions about your health
   d. All of the above
5. A PHP helps your DOCTOR know
   a. Who you are
   b. Where you have been
   c. What you have done, and what needs to be done
   d. All of the above

Answers:
   1. D   2. A   3. C   4. D   5. D

References

Cohen, E. (2009). How to avoid falling victim to a hospital mistake. CNN. http://www.cnn.com/2009/HEALTH/11/11/hospital.mistakes/index.html, accessed November 17, 2009.

Rankin, S. H., Stallings, K. D. and London, F. (2005). *Patient Education in Health and Illness* (5th edn.). Philadelphia, PA: Lippincott Williams & Wilkins. 119. www.notimetoteach.com

Rys, R. (2008). The imposter in the ER." *Health care on NBC News.com*. March 13, 2008. http://www.msnbc.msn.com/id/23392229

Tesh, J. (2009). Patients who communicate well with their doctors are healthier. *Health & Well-Being*. John Tesh: Intelligence for Your Life. May 18, 2009. http://www.tesh.com/ittrium/visit?path=A1xc797x1y1xa5x1x76y1x241fx1x9by1x2424x1y5x1ae88x5x1

Chapter 10

PHP Instructor Materials:
How to Use Your PHP

Power can be taken, but not given. The process of the taking is empowerment in itself.

Gloria Steinem
American activist

Learning Objectives

1. Comprehend the dynamics and purpose of a healthcare portfolio
2. Acknowledge the complexity of healthcare
3. Understand patient-centric care
4. Recognize ways to protect your physical and fiscal health
5. Introduce the concept of self-advocacy

What Exactly Is a Personal Healthcare Portfolio?

A healthcare portfolio is a patient-centric health data management model. The job of the patient advocate is to work with patients as they navigate the use of this model. In addition, the patient advocate is poised to be a conduit to assess an individual's readiness to assemble their health information, validate it, and understand it, followed by being in a position to use it to advocate for themselves within the healthcare system.

Why Does a Patient Need One?

A patient cannot make the right decision without the right data at the right time. This Personal Healthcare Portfolio (PHP) model is structured to create a personal health data management plan. Once a patient has control of their information, the next steps are to understand the complexities of the healthcare system and seek the care needed, at a reasonable cost. The PHP model engages the individual in continuing to update their PHP with new information as they navigate the healthcare system. This chapter will go into detail on how to do so with the help of a PHP.

What Will the Result of Using Your PHP Look Like?

1. **Improve and simplify your healthcare**
   a. Direct and control your healthcare experiences
   b. Become a conscientious consumer of healthcare
   c. Manage family healthcare records
   d. Share medical information with doctors and insurance companies
2. **Assemble your healthcare facts (including health, wellness, financial, and health assessment-related aspects)**
   a. Make informed decisions about your healthcare
   b. Receive the best healthcare possible
   c. Manage, control, and reduce your healthcare costs
   d. Prevent adverse healthcare outcomes
   e. Safeguard your protected health information

Patient Message: Without a PHP, you have a real risk of being subjected to medical and financial errors as well as fraud, waste, and abuse. By contrast, using a PHP will help you be your own best advocate. It will help remove the complexity, uncertainty, and stress from your healthcare experiences *and* save you money.

Patient Instruction Example

In the investment world, a portfolio is a collection of your investments. In the art world, a portfolio can be a collection of your paintings, sculptures, photographs, and drawings. Your PHP is a collection of all of the information related to your healthcare. You probably have compiled more health information over your lifetime than you think. Such information is found in all the records and documents having anything to do with your medical care, health insurance, or prescription drug history. It is found in patient records, billing statements, wellness plans, treatment plans, health benefit plans, and insurance information.

As mentioned, your PHP is your personal health record. Be careful not to confuse it with an electronic health record (EHR). An EHR is a digital document generated by a special computer network utilized by healthcare providers to record your treatments and health information to document your care. Your PHP, however, is owned and controlled by *you* and comprises the information you collect about yourself and from your providers.

Patient Instruction Example: Why Do You Need a Personal Healthcare Portfolio?

By continuously updating your PHP, you take an active role in your healthcare. Keep your PHP up to date by adding health information *every time* you visit a doctor, nurse practitioner, psychologist, *or any other healthcare service provider*. Keep the information in a simple and organized portfolio. It should be available to you when and where you need it. It should even prepare you for your upcoming appointments, track changes in your health status, and be accessible in case of emergency. If properly organized and updated, your PHP will help you to

- Take control of your healthcare
  - Live a healthy life and record your progress
  - Make better care decisions
  - Empower yourself to be an informed healthcare consumer
- The benefit of having a PHP at your fingertips can make the difference between life and death, as well as save you time and money
  - No more time wasted searching for your records (have them at your fingertips at appointments, while traveling, and when your doctors' offices are closed).
  - Communicate faster and more accurately with your doctor (no longer waste time answering 10-page questionnaires each time you visit a new healthcare provider).
  - Have the ability to monitor your bills.

Complexity of Healthcare

There are countless numbers of professionals, companies, organizations, and government agencies involved in healthcare today. It is very easy to feel confused and overwhelmed when dealing with these entities.

Reason: Healthcare is not delivered to patients in a manner that is transparent and straightforward. One episode of healthcare can feel like being trapped in a maze. It can involve many zigzags, bends, curves, turns, and roundabouts, with no end in sight.

Example: When you go to a hospital for surgery, you are admitted, have the procedure, and are then sent home. Usually, you are not told how much the surgery is going to cost when you arrive at the hospital—and you are not handed a bill when you leave. Getting healthcare is not like going to your grocery store. When you walk into a store and fill your cart with groceries, you must pay for these groceries before you leave and the transaction ends when the cashier hands you your receipt.

Contrast: The paperwork related to your surgery can begin long before you even get to the hospital. It may not conclude until well after you leave. Your surgery generates all sorts of information and financial transactions. These transactions can occur between many parties, including doctors, hospitals, insurance companies and their networks, third-party administrators, employers, government agencies, pharmacies, pharmacy benefit managers, case managers, therapists, hospices, attorneys, medical technicians, pharmaceutical manufacturers, etc. However, in emergency situations, doctors and patients may feel rushed to make decisions with the information that is immediately available. Imagine an active real-time healthcare portfolio that allows patients and their healthcare professionals to access all information in real time. This is the wave of the future.

The good news: While healthcare is often exceedingly complicated, it does not have to be that way. Health decisions that are made without all the facts are the main driver of adverse, drawn-out, and possibly deadly results. The best decisions of your life were probably made with all of the relevant facts at hand. Having an understanding of your health and financially related information is vital to making the right decisions about your health.

Patient Message: Right now, your health information is most likely not in one place that you can easily access. The experts are still debating healthcare delivery. In the meantime, take control of your own information!

Patient-Centric Care

For years, experts have suggested that patient-centric care is a key ingredient to the improvement of our healthcare system.

What it means: Patient-centric care is all about the patient's own interests and needs being the center of their own healthcare experience. In a patient-centric system, the success of healthcare depends to some extent on patient engagement. As our healthcare system gradually shifts to a patient-centric mode, the patient will become more responsible for their own well-being and treatment. Patient-centric care is becoming more feasible due to advances in technology as well as economic pressures to contain healthcare costs.

Patient Message: Your PHP will arm you with the information needed to be a responsible, conscientious consumer of healthcare services. Your PHP will also enable providers to review all of your health information not within their system, allowing then to present better options about your care.

Patient Instruction Example (1)

Remember, as a healthcare consumer, your **rights** include the

1. *Right to information* in a timely fashion, in a form that you can easily understand.
2. *Right to a choice of healthcare providers* that are qualified to ensure appropriate high-quality care.
3. *Right to access emergency health services* when and where the need arises.
4. *Right to be involved in any decision*-making processes related to your healthcare.
5. *Right to considerate, respectful care* from all members of the healthcare system at all times and under any circumstance.
6. *Right to communicate* with doctors with confidentiality regarding all your individually identifiable healthcare information.
7. *Right to a process* in which you can communicate disputes and receive a response with a qualified, competent, and independent review of your complaint.

As a patient, you also have the following responsibilities:

1. *Adopt* healthy habits and become directly involved in your healthcare decisions.
2. *Work* collaboratively with your doctors to develop and carry out agreed-upon treatment plans.
3. *Use* your health plan's internal complaint and appeal process to address concerns.
4. *Recognize* the reality of the risks and limits of science and human capabilities.
5. *Become* knowledgeable about your insurance and/or health plan coverage and policies, and follow rules and procedures.
6. *Make* a good faith effort to meet financial obligations.
7. *Report* fraud and wrongdoing.

Patient Message: Make sure you exercise your rights and understand your responsibilities. View your PHP as an investment in yourself. The more complex your health issues are, the more likely it is that you are going to face financial and emotional distress in dealing with them. The use of your PHP to manage and coordinate your healthcare (and the information related to your healthcare) will allow you to advocate for yourself. Having a PHP means having your facts when you need them. That will spare you much of the anguish that you would be forced to endure without it. You may feel as if you do not have enough time, energy, or understanding to take an active role in your healthcare. Do not be intimidated. There are professional resources that you and your loved ones can turn to for help.

Patient Instruction Example (2)

Patient advocates help people take charge of their healthcare. They help people collect, understand, and use their medical and financial information to make good healthcare decisions. They also help people pay medical bills, review insurance and/or health plans, sign up for Medicare, obtain priority referrals (and pursue convenient access to healthcare), monitor for medical identity theft, and resolve other concerns related to their healthcare.

Patient Message: Know your rights and responsibilities; online resources such as the Centers for Medicaid and Medicare Services under consumer resources at cms.gov will provide the most recent listing of patient considerations. In addition, most States have online resources within the Department of Health and or Department of Insurance.

Protecting Health and Finances with a PHP

As discussed previously, our healthcare system is made up of many fragmented participants—hospitals, doctors, clinics, insurance companies, employers, and government-sponsored programs (including Medicare and Medicaid). These entities do not share all of your healthcare information, which is why it is often so difficult to obtain timely, appropriate healthcare without payment disputes.

Example: A patient may see several different doctors at multiple locations. The services received may be paid for by multiple parties—the insurance company, an independent health plan, a government program in which the patient is enrolled, or the patient themselves.

Problem: Providers are often unaware of another provider's treatment plan for the patient. This lack of communication results in medical errors, financial errors and fraud, waste, and abuse.

The Institute of Medicine estimates that about 100,000 Americans die each year from preventable medical errors. About one-fifth of these errors are the result of a lack of immediate access to patient health information. Moreover, recent disasters (including Hurricane Katrina) have caused thousands of medical records to literally disappear.

Real Examples of Medical Errors

- A doctor operated on and amputated the wrong leg of a veteran.
- An elderly woman received the wrong blood type during a blood transfusion.
- A young adult died after a hospital served him a food product that he was allergic to.
- A CT scan performed on a pregnant woman with a similar name to a patient complaining of abdominal pain resulted in harm to the unborn baby.

The annual price tag for medical errors, according to the Agency for Healthcare Research and Quality, is $37.6 billion. That's about *$4.3 million per hour.*

Preventable medical errors may cost the United States up to $1 trillion dollars in lost human potential and contributions, according to the *Journal of Health Care Finance* article "The Economics of Healthcare Quality and Medical Errors"* (Charles Andel, 2012). Previous studies show the economic impact to range from $17 billion to $50 billion annually, focused only on direct medical costs such as ancillary services, prescription drug services, and inpatient/outpatient care. Author Stephen Davidow noted that "previous studies do not come close to illustrating the economic loss of human potential and contribution, which families, colleagues, businesses and communities experience when someone dies from a preventable medical error." On a human level, the effect of poor quality care is incalculable. The authors developed an approach based on quality-adjusted life years (QALYs) to attempt a calculation of the effect of errors. Based on studies by the Institute of Medicine (IOM) and others, there is a loss of $73.5–$98 billion in QALYs. It is believed, however, that preventable deaths due to medical errors are 10 times higher than the IOM estimate—an economic impact loss of $735 billion–$980 billion—amounting to nearly $1 trillion. And when you factor in the lost productivity of patients who survive a medical error but are disabled for an extended period of time, the economic impact could be much greater.

Real Examples of Financial Errors

- Billing patients for services never received.
- Billing patients more than once for the same service(s).
- Billing patients for related procedures that should be bundled separately (this practice is known as "unbundling charges"). In a fancy restaurant, it is referred to as *à la carte pricing* when the menu states that the salad is included with the entree.

The annual price tag for financial errors, according to the Centers for Medicare and Medicaid Services, is $108 billion—or 16% of the total spent **by government programs.** That's about *$12.3 million per hour.*

Note: **In Chapter 9, section entitled "Reality of Healthcare for Payers,"** the statement "When you combine the volume of claims processed by private payer systems and third-party administrators for our government programs, the amount of money being lost to fraud, waste, and abuse is estimated at about $400,000 per minute. That is $210.2 billion per year" does not include the amount of money that is associated with waste and abuse in healthcare. The tab for waste and abuse is estimated to be closer to 10% each. Imagine what we can do with those dollars if they are spent appropriately.

---

* Andel. C., Davidow. S.L., Hollander. M., Moreno. D.A. *J Health Care Finance.* 2012; 39: 39–50, accessed 1/27/16.

Real Examples of Fraud, Waste, and Abuse

- Fake salesmen/brokers selling fake insurance cards to unsuspecting consumers who think they have purchased health insurance but where the perpetrators just steal the premiums instead of paying healthcare claims
- Providing medically unnecessary services
- Stealing patient identities; enrolled patients selling their insurance cards
- Selling counterfeit drugs
- Submitting fraudulent insurance claims for services never rendered

According to the National Center for Policy Analysis, Medicare pays $33 billion dollars for fraudulent services each year.* According to a Blue Cross Blue Shield report, insurance companies pay another $50 billion for fraudulent services. The annual total price tag for fraud, waste, and abuse activity is a whopping $83 billion, or approximately *$9.4 million per hour*.

For additional information on medical and financial errors and fraud, waste, and abuse, send your question to info@mbaaudit.com.

Here are sample questions from patients:

Got Fraud?

Sample Question: "My doctor's bill for my spinal fusion was $97,000, but my hospital bill was only $37,000. How could the doctor's bill be so much more expensive than the hospital's bill?"

Answer: Review all of your bills. Understand Current Procedural Terminology (CPT) codes. CPT is a numeric system for all medical procedures. Doctors and healthcare professionals use these codes to get paid. Upon review of the bills, it looks like the doctor charged his surgery fee three times: once under his name, again under his physician assistant's name, and a third time under an assistant surgeon's name. This practice is questionable, may result in over billing. Call your insurance carrier and or contact an advocate who specializes in auditing healthcare claims.

Got Health?

---

* Herrick, D. M. Medicare drug plans need the tools to fight prescription drug fraud. National Center for Policy Analysis, Policy Report no. 359.

Sample Question: "My doctor has me on Ponstan for my arthritis, and lately my pain has been getting worse—especially my kidneys (lower back pain). Does this drug have an effect on my kidneys?"

Answer: This drug tends to affect the heart and gastrointestinal system—not your kidneys. The problem is that there is a lot of counterfeit Ponstan on the market. Look at Figure 10.1. Although similar in appearance to the authentic tablet on the right, the counterfeit Ponstan tablet on the left does not contain active ingredients. *Instead, it is composed of boric acid, brick dust, and paint.* Boric acid is a pesticide that can cause gastrointestinal problems and renal failure. If you suspect that your medicine is not the real thing, immediately take your prescription back to your pharmacist. Ask your pharmacy to evaluate the medication that they provided to you. *Do not return the entire bottle.* Keep the remaining pills to show to your doctor in an immediate follow-up to evaluate the seriousness of your condition.

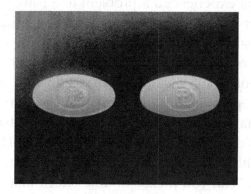

Illustration 1. Can you tell the difference?

Patient Message: Healthcare is a trillion dollar market and the crooks are looking for you and your money. Please be safe.

Patient Example Instruction: Self-Advocacy

When you are armed with a PHP, you can record and track your healthcare on a continuous basis. Your PHP captures every step that you take within the healthcare system. Your PHP records those steps in a manageable format so that you have your health information ready and accessible whenever you need it. Just like a photo album, your PHP keeps a record of large and small events and tells the complete story of your health.

This book is also a starting point for professionals involved in patient advocacy and for individuals to learn how to advocate for themselves. Invest in continuous healthcare education—there are ample opportunities to do so.

Example: Take courses on healthcare support and wellness programs at reputable organizations, including classes at your local area healthcare facilities, universities, and established patient education organizations.

Examples of Self-Advocacy

Example: **Avoid clinical errors by having your information organized in an efficient manner.** Patty, a patient, did not know until she had her first surgery that she had unusual reactions to anesthesia—she experienced intraoperative awakening. In other words, she was paralyzed but unfortunately awake during surgery. She reported this and her doctor told her she was dreaming. The reality was that this syndrome runs in her family. Patty was instructed by her advocate to get a copy of the anesthesia record. She carried it in her PHP. Thereafter, prior to any future surgery, she had the anesthesiologist look at it prior to signing a consent form. Guess what? She never experienced it again in her subsequent surgeries and the doctors who performed the operations thanked her for providing them with this important information.

Example: **Learn how to avoid being a victim of medical errors and complications.** If you experienced a problem like Patty—in which you were awake while in surgery or any other complication—get the actual record showing the complication so your next doctor can be informed to avoid the same mistake. This will be one record you will want your next provider to have.

Case study: Patient "Tom" walked out of his doctors' appointment. He checked out with reception and asked what CPT code he was being charged for. The receptionist hesitantly stated, "99215." He asked, "What does CPT 99215 represent?" She said, "Established outpatient visit—40 min." He paused and asked, "But I was not with the doctor for 40 min. I was only with him for 15 min." He followed up with, "Can you please double-check that before I leave?" Most patients never really know the official code that the doctor is using, if ever. The difference between a 40 minute visit and a 15 minute visit was $200.

Patient Message: CPT is a coding system that indicates *what* was done to a patient. Another coding system, the International Classification of Diseases (ICD), is the diagnosis coding system, or *why* the service was performed. Every time you leave a hospital or a doctor's office, the service provider records at least one ICD code and at least one CPT code. Even your pharmacy records an ICD code with the prescription you obtain. This occurs even when you buy medical supplies, such as a wheelchair. Basically, the codes tell your health plan (insurance company) what the providers did and why they did it. Next time you leave your provider's office, use these terms like Tom did and ask at checkout: "By the way, what CPT code was I charged for today?" Providers know that if the patient is watching, they must be careful not to try to leverage the system.

Example: **Don't let providers keep you in the dark about your treatment options.** Sandra was being treated for breast cancer. She was offered one treatment option. Unknown to her, this particular cancer treatment center used the same chemotherapy treatment option for all of its breast cancer patients. Coincidently, the chemotherapy treatment she was prescribed happened to be the treatment that had the highest reimbursement amount for the provider. This financially driven healthcare offering aspect of the market is rarely transparent to patients. Fortunately for Sandra, through her patient advocate, she learned not only to get a second opinion but to also ask *upfront* what her health plan (insurance company) will typically pay for each option and which ones they will not pay for. In addition, she asked the providers about the different types of chemotherapy treatment they tended to provide (which is a different question from "what chemotherapy do you recommend?") and how much they charged for each. It is no different from a computer salesman trying to sell you a laptop with the highest commission. The crazy part of healthcare, though, is that the patient has to watch the payer (who coincidently recommends the least expensive option) and at the same time watch out for the provider (who coincidently recommends the option in which they make the most money). Unfortunately, it is a "buyer-beware" market.

Example: **Know your rights and responsibilities, and avoid paperwork errors.** Patient "Steve" was distracted, thinking about his health versus paper work while he had ongoing treatment for cancer. He utilized his patient advocate to ensure that his disability benefits were protected through his employer by making sure the paperwork was filled out correctly and in a timely fashion. If not, he would have lost the coverage he needed to get his treatment.

Example: **Don't leave your doctor's appointments until you have all of the details you need about your medications, goals, or treatment plans.** Patient "Joan" was in her eighties and her children were always concerned about making sure she understood her doctors' instructions. Her advocate trained her children to help their mother write down her questions before her doctors' visits. During the visits, she used her forms to write down her doctors' instructions. With a proper health release (a consent form providing permission for access to information) in hand, her children were able to follow up with the doctor to make sure Joan went home with a full understanding of what she was supposed to do.

Patient Message: Self advocacy is about knowing how to ask the right questions at the right time to make the right decision.

Patient Example Instruction

PHP Checklist (see PHP templates in Section III)

- Do you need a PHP? Do you have your complete healthcare history written down?
- If not, do you know where to begin to get all of your health information?
- Do you know if all of your doctors have all of your information?
- Do you know your rights as a patient?
- Are you aware of free resources to protect yourself as a patient?
- Do you have a plan if you cannot advocate for yourself?
- Do you know how to ensure that you receive the best possible care?

If you answered no to any of these questions, then you'll want to consider getting one.

Future of Healthcare

Healthcare reform has been a focus for the federal government for decades. Change, however, does not happen overnight. In fact, in the words of George Bernard Shaw, "The reasonable man adapts himself to the world; the unreasonable man persists in trying to adapt the world to himself. Therefore, all progress depends on the unreasonable man." As the reasonable men of Congress continue their 100-year struggle with defining and revising our healthcare system, "unreasonable" consumers must take charge of their own health.

Congress has been making changes to U.S. healthcare since 1901. As a result, it is safe to say that we will continue to see significant or incremental revisions and positive changes to our healthcare system from the use of information technology and EHRs. This is, for the most part, a good thing as it will result in fewer deaths derived from medical errors as well as opportunities to reduce costs.

President George W. Bush called for the U.S. healthcare industry to embrace EHRs. U.S. President Barack Obama called for "this Congress to finally pass the legislation we need to better meet the evolving threat of cyber attacks, combat identity theft and protect our children's information. If we don't act, we'll leave our nation and our economy vulnerable." The impact of the Affordable Care Act has been significant. The market has responded, both good and bad, and we expect that change will continue to occur.

Significant inroads are being initiated in healthcare technology through the Department of Health and Human Services under the Health Information Technology program. You can learn about it at www.hhs.gov/healthit.* However, we still face enormous challenges in getting doctors to fully implement EHRs and patients to receive and manage their information electronically. It is therefore difficult to predict when information technology will be the norm versus the exception in our healthcare system. In the meantime, your PHP enables you to be in control of your healthcare information and protect yourself from the system's many flaws and traps *right now*.

Patient Message: You must take care of yourself NOW, while Congress and other stake holders continue to figure it out and continue to make changes.

Patient Example Instruction: What to Include in Your PHP?

Your PHP should be divided into five major sections: Health, Wellness, Financial, Personal Assessments, and a Document Manager. Use each section to collect, record, store, and manage personal information related to your healthcare. Included within your PHP should be places to record and store

---

* *Electronic Health Records An Audit and Internal Control Guide*, John Wiley, page 20.

- Your personal information, to be used at the time of registration
- A list of your significant illnesses and operations
- A list of medications that you take
- A list of allergies that you have
- Progress notes, opinions, and physician orders from your doctors
- Laboratory and x-ray test results
- Immunization records
- Insurance documents
- Medical bills
- Consent and authorization forms
- Other documents related to your healthcare experience.

Please note that the introductory PHP attached to this book in Section III has a step-by-step guide to each of the items in this list. The remaining chapters in this book provide specific guidelines to help the patient use a PHP and take control of their healthcare.

Study Questions

1. Who are you able to share your PHP with?
   a. A doctor
   b. An employer
   c. A real estate agent
   d. Credit card companies
2. PHP is a collection of all but ONE of these:
   a. Billing statements
   b. Veterinary records
   c. Treatment plans
   d. Insurance information
3. Which of the following is NOT a reason to improve and simplify your healthcare?
   a. Manage and control your healthcare expenses
   b. Become a conscientious consumer of healthcare
   c. Manage family healthcare records
   d. Share medical information with coworkers
4. What is a reason to assemble your PHP?
   a. To receive the best healthcare possible
   b. To prevent adverse healthcare outcomes
   c. To make informed decisions about your healthcare
   d. All of the above

5. What will a PHP provide you with?
    a. The potential to become a victim of fraud
    b. A loss of income
    c. A loss of medical coverage
    d. Better healthcare while saving you money

Answer Key:
1. A   2. B   3. D   4. D   5. D

Chapter 11

PHP Instructor Materials: Your Personal Health Information

Information is a source of learning, but unless it is organized, processed, and available to the right people in a format for decision making, it is a burden, not a benefit.

William Pollard
English clergyman 1828–1893

Learning Objectives

1. Understand what a medical record is
2. Understand how to request and obtain your health information
3. Understand healthcare privacy
4. Understand the use of several healthcare forms: medical record request, consent for release of information, medical record discrepancy form, power of attorney (POA)

This chapter is dedicated to material that should be considered when working with individuals as an advocate.

Patient Instruction Example: Your Medical Records

As discussed earlier, healthcare is extremely fragmented between your different providers, your insurance company, health records with your employer, pharmacy records, supply records, and the list goes on. The volume of information collected can easily overwhelm you, so keep a steady focus on the task at hand, knowing you have a right to your information, and be persistent in obtaining it.

Keep in mind that your doctor will generate a progress note of each visit in a medical record or file. These notes describe their assessment of your condition and the treatment they are recommending/providing to you. Doctors also include details of all diagnostic tests or lab work they have requested for you, as well as their results, in your medical record. Finally, doctors add their consultation notes. Consultation notes reflect the advice one healthcare provider gives to another about your case.

Example: Imagine you are seeing a heart doctor, who notices something is wrong with your lungs. Your heart doctor may contact your pulmonary doctor (a lung specialist) and talk over the treatment options that could be available to you relative to your heart condition.

Patient Message: Your information is out there, so start tracking it down, one source at a time.

Gathering and Using Your Personal Health Information[1]

Each time you receive care, your doctors create a record of your visit. Each doctor compiles a separate file with information about you. Your doctors use your information to monitor health, coordinate care, and generate the billing for your treatment. If your information is used for any other purpose, such as research, your provider must disclose this in a consent form.

Recording of your health information starts at the time you register for services. Registration personnel collect your personal and financial information and your method of payment. Your information then moves to the treatment section. Here, your doctor (treatment provider) gathers information about your health status, including

- Medical history
- Physical exam and condition
- Progress reports
- Physician orders
- Labs, tests, and surgeries
- Any other provider records of past treatments

Your health information then moves to the medical records department. This department is responsible for keeping your information private while storing the paper and electronic information. Next, your diagnosis and insurance information is sent to the patient accounts or billing departments. Here, your benefit information is processed so that you can be billed for the services you received.

Doctors and hospitals are also responsible for reporting certain types of information to third parties, such as public health agencies. Ask your provider to inform you if any information is released and, if so, specifically which pieces of information were involved. Certain agencies use your information to track community illness and quality of care improvement. Your information could also be sent to law enforcement personnel under certain circumstances.

If you have insurance, your information is sent from the patient accounts or billing department (usually electronically) to your insurance company. Your provider and your insurance company may exchange your health information to verify the services provided to you. Your employers also may have access to your records in some circumstances. For example, if you have a work-related injury, your employer's case management department (or those in charge of managing workers' compensation) may have created a file of the incident.

If you have insurance through your employer, it is important to understand whether or not the plan is self-insured, which means that the company pays for all employee healthcare services—*not* the insurance company. Self-insured plans are governed by a federal statute called the Employee Retirement Income Security Act (ERISA). Some employers purchase insurance coverage for employees. If you have insurance through a third-party health insurance company, the plan is regulated by the department of insurance for your state.

If you are unsure what kind of plan your employer subscribes to, ask your human resources department for information about your plan.

Key: Understanding the type of plan you have also helps you understand your rights. For example, if your employer is self-insured, the plan most likely is governed by ERISA rules. So if you have a problem or dispute over payment for healthcare services, you will most likely be required to go through the appeal process administered by the health plan. If your employer has insurance then the plan is subject to state law, which means that if you want to appeal a claim, you must submit your concern to the department of insurance for the state you live in.

Patient Message: Understand how your information is being used. Simply ask: What are you doing with my information, and why do you need it?

Obtaining Your Records

It is critically important to understand that the information contained in your medical records *belongs to you*. Your providers own your actual medical record, but *you* are the owner of the information within your medical record.

Healthy people generally see a doctor once a year for an evaluation, as well as occasional visits for other minor ailments. These people should request a copy of their records once a year.

If you are suffering from a protracted illness, request copies of your records every quarter as people with an active illness will see their doctors more often. If you have a chronic condition such as diabetes or asthma, you should request your records twice per year.

Most efficient: Contact your doctor's office or the medical records department at the facility where you received care and request copies of your medical records. Some facilities will give you your information in an electronic format. Most will make paper copies for you, but be aware that you may be charged for these. Many facilities will also charge you for supplies, labor, and any postage necessary to provide you with your records.

Make sure that you request and receive *all* parts of your medical records, regardless of the format in which the information is delivered to you. Providers may only send you an "abstract" that includes the general sections of your medical records such as progress notes, diagnostic labs and tests, and consultation notes. Be sure to specifically request all documentation, including billing information as well as the claim forms to be submitted to the insurance company. If you also want information that is kept by your health plan (insurance carrier), contact their customer service department in order to obtain a copy of their file, which is separate from the provider's file.

Note: Some records (especially immunization records) can be difficult to obtain because your doctors may have changed locations, retired, or died. However, all doctors are required to save patient records for a period defined by federal and state law (typically 7 years). If you are having trouble locating any of your providers, try contacting your healthcare provider's partners, local medical society, state medical association, or the state's department of health.

When you request and receive your medical records, check them to make sure that the record includes the treatment you actually received. Be aware that it can take 30–60 days to receive your medical records, so remember to ask when you should expect to receive the information that you requested. Let your provider know immediately if you need your records prior to treatment from another doctor so his office can expedite the process.

Patient Message: Keep track of your information at regular intervals, or if necessary, as it is being generated. By doing so, information can be validated and used in real time.

Ensuring Accuracy

Review your medical records carefully to make sure that they are accurate and complete. Under the Health Insurance Portability Accountability Act (HIPAA), you have the right to submit an amendment request to your provider. The amendment request should identify anything inaccurate that you noted within your records. Make sure to document in writing any inaccurate information and provide the correct information that should be in your record. (To learn more about your rights under HIPAA, visit www.hhs.gov/ocr/hipaa.)

Doctors must respond or acknowledge your request to amend your records within 30 days. They will have two choices: (1) to update your medical record to reflect your amendment or (2) to explain why they will not change your medical record. When doctors decide not to change your medical record, they must place the submitted request for amendment in a file with your medical record.

Also, make certain that you thoroughly review your lab and test results so you can make sure that you have been informed about all findings, regardless of the outcomes. If you find something that does not seem right or that is unfamiliar to you, request verification that the tests actually belong to you. Schedule an appointment with your doctor immediately to resolve any concerns. Horror stories in which cancer patients are not informed of their diagnoses, for whatever reason, are more common than you would think.

The privacy rules guaranteeing access to your medical records constitute one of the most important patient rights provided under HIPAA. Make sure to take full advantage of them. *Here is an example of why*:

EXAMPLE

A 36-year-old woman named Sheila sought out her patient advocate because health insurers were consistently turning her down for coverage and she wanted to know why. Sheila had a history of occasional heart palpitations and her cardiologist, Dr. Carl, treated her for a heart disorder called *mitral valve prolapse*. He told Sheila that she eventually might want to get an echocardiogram (an assessment of the heart). She agreed, but together they decided that it was not necessary to have it done yet because she had no active symptoms.

The answer to Sheila's problem became apparent upon review of her medical records. Sheila's medical records did not accurately reflect what she had shared with her advocate. Her medical record read "patient refused test against medical advice." The doctor's note made it look like Sheila was a noncompliant patient, so her advocate helped her submit a request for an amendment. Sheila discussed with her doctor why he made that statement. He apologized and stated, "I was documenting, defensive medicine style." The doctor did not want to be in a position to get sued, so he was writing his notes "defensively." Dr. Carl changed his notes to reflect the actual conversation and Sheila was able to obtain health insurance without further difficulty.

Sheila's story illustrates how important it is to take ownership of your health information and to remember to review your medical records carefully and periodically.

If your doctor does not respond to your request, then you may file a formal complaint through the U.S. Department of Health and Human Services (DHHS):

U.S. Department of Health and Human Services Office of Civil Rights, 200 Independence Avenue, S.W. Washington, D.C., 20201 (866)627-7748, www.hhs.gov.

For the regional office nearest you, e-mail OCRComplaint@hhs.gov or visit www.hhs.gov/ocr/hipaahealth.txt.

Privacy Concerns

Federal law protects the privacy of your health information. HIPAA protects the maintenance and transmission of your "individually identifiable health information (IIHI)." IIHI is information that identifies who you are. It may include information about your physical and mental health and the receipt and payment of your healthcare services, as well as your participation in your health plan. HIPAA protects your information whether it is communicated in writing, electronically, or in verbal form.

Your health plan (insurance) must provide you with a Notice of Privacy Practice. This notice explains how your information is being used and who has access to it. Your doctors may also give you a copy of their Notice of Privacy Practice to read. If they do not, ask for one. They will usually ask you to sign a document that acknowledges that you have received notice of your right to privacy.*

You and your provider share responsibility to (1) give an accurate account of your health history to your healthcare providers, (2) know what information is being released when you authorize the release of your information and to whom it is being released, and (3) ensure that the information in your health record is complete and accurate.[2]

Unauthorized disclosure of sensitive information does happen and, as mentioned in earlier chapters, medical identity theft is a growing concern.[3] You must take an active role in protecting your privacy.

Patient Message: Treat and protect your health information in the same manner as you do your bank and credit card information.

Privacy in Your Pharmacy

As the trend grows for doctors to submit prescriptions electronically, the risk of unauthorized access to your records will increase.

Effective Approach: Request privacy and security policies from your pharmacy so that you know who is seeing your prescription records and how that information is being protected.[4]

Important: Insurance companies do not send you an explanation of the benefits report regarding pharmacy charges submitted in your name to your insurance company. From time to time, contact your insurance company and ask for a claim run on medications charged to your name.

Privacy: Myths versus Reality

Health information privacy laws are complicated and often misinterpreted. Below are some common privacy myths, as noted by the American Health Information Management Association (AHIMA) at www.ahima.org:

1. **Myth:** Your doctors need your consent to disclose personal health information to another doctor, family member, or other third parties.
   Reality: Your doctors may share your personal health information with other doctors "if there is a reason to believe you will receive care there." They may share it with or without your authorization with a spouse, parent, or child who is involved in your care if you are unable to consent to the

---

* "Notice of Privacy Practices."

disclosure. Your information may also be used for research purposes or as a legal document when evidence of care is needed.

2. **Myth:** Your doctors cannot leave a voice mail for you or a message with someone else who answers your phone.

   Reality: Your doctors can leave you a voice mail if your outgoing message states your name or number for verification, and can leave a message with someone else with your consent.

3. **Myth:** Your health information cannot be faxed or e-mailed.

   Reality: Your health information can be faxed if the organization has a secured encrypted process. It can be e-mailed if the sender has a method of protecting the transmitted health information from unauthorized access (such as encryption and decryption).

4. **Myth:** Hospitals may not give out your name and location during your hospitalization without your consent.

   Reality: You must specifically ask *not* to be listed in a hospital's directory if you do not want it known that you are a patient there.

5. **Myth:** You do not have access to your child's medical records.

   There are only three occasions in which the statement above is generally true:

   a. Parental consent is not required under law for your child to receive care
   b. Your child obtains care at the guidance of a court or person appointed by the court
   c. When you agree that your child and the attending doctor have a confidential relationship

   Reality: Even in these circumstances, however, parents may receive access if allowed by the law.

6. **Myth:** You are legally barred from access to your parent's health record.

   Reality: If you want access to your parent's health record, you must have your parent submit a written authorization letter to each doctor and facility involved in his or her care. If your parent agrees to release their health information to you, make sure the language in the authorization letter expressively says so. You will need to give this authorization letter to each doctor's office and the health information management department at each facility.

If you think that someone has violated your privacy, contact your doctor's office or the privacy officer at the facility where you believe the violation occurred. If you are unable to resolve your concern, you can file a formal complaint about the violator to the Department of Health and Human Services' Office for Civil Rights (OCR). You must file a complaint within 180 days of when the violation came to your attention. For more information, visit the OCR Web site (www.hhs.gov/ocr/hipaa) or contact a patient advocate.

Patient Message: Know your privacy rights and how to protect yourself if your health information has been compromised.

Sample Medical Record Request and Consent Forms

This section includes a sample based on forms used by Medical Business Associates' patient advocates:

- Letter to send to your doctor or hospital to request copies of your medical records (Appendix 11.1).
- Letter for your patient advocate (or designated representative) to use to request records on your behalf (Appendix 11.2).
- Letter to send if you find a discrepancy in your record that you would like amended. Visit www.mbaaudit.com (info@mbaaudit.com) for additional forms and support.

Important: Your request for information must be submitted in the correct format to be considered.

APPENDIX 11.1: MEDICAL RECORD REQUEST FORM

[Date]
To: [Provider Name
       Provider Address]
Re: [Patient Name
       Date of Birth
       Social Security Number]

Dear [Provider Name]:

Enclosed please find a release of information and consent from the above patient.

I request the following information:

_____ UB04 (facility) or CMS 1500 (professional) form for each healthcare episode.

_____ The itemized bill for each healthcare episode.

_____ A complete copy of the medical records. (Please do not forward an abstract. Send a complete copy of all documents, including any ancillary department records on this patient.)

_____ Any electronic records that are not maintained in hard-copy form.

Please forward the information to [your address].

Please contact me at [your contact information] with any questions or concerns.

Sincerely,
[Your name]

APPENDIX 11.2: CONSENT FOR RELEASE OF INFORMATION FORM

CONFIDENTIAL AUTHORIZATION

I authorize_____

To provide_____

with information (electronic, fax, and/or photocopy) concerning healthcare or treatment provided to the patient, employee, or deceased named below. This may include information relating to mental illness, communicable or infectious diseases, HIV testing, acquired immune deficiency syndrome (AIDS), AIDS-related complex, use of drugs or alcohol, etc.

The following information is requested:

_____Teleconferences with the provider or payer.

_____An on-site appointment to review the original records.

_____A **complete** copy of all records, including patient medical record documents, films, DVDs, ancillary department reports, procedure reports, physician orders, consults, general notes, and billing statements. (Please do not forward an abstract of the medical record.) Please include copies of records received by other providers.

_____All billing information, including itemized bill(s), respective applicable CMS 1500 or UB 04 form (formerly UB 92), and carrier correspondence.

This authorization is valid from the date signed and for a period of 2 years thereafter unless revoked by me or by my legal representative in writing. I agree that a copy of this authorization shall be as valid as the original.

_____	_____	_____
Name of Patient	Date of Birth	Social Security #

(If the patient is able to sign, please fill in the blank fields in section 1 below. If the patient is a minor, deceased, adjudged incompetent, or otherwise unable to sign, please fill in all blank fields in section 2 below.)

1. _____   _____
   Date of signature   Signature of patient

2. _____   _____
   Date of signature   *Person authorized to sign for the patient

_____   _____
Relationship to patient   Reason patient is unable to sign

*Note: Persons authorized to sign for the patient generally include the parent, guardian, or legal custodian of a minor patient; the guardian or conservator of a patient judged incompetent; the personal representative or spouse of deceased patient; or any person authorized in writing by the patient. If you have any questions about this form, you may contact me at [your contact information].

Study Questions

1. What is included in your medical records?
   a. Progress notes describing your condition and treatment
   b. Details and results of diagnostic tests and lab work
   c. Consultation notes
   d. All of the above
2. Who has records of visits to your doctor's office?
   a. Doctors and pharmacists
   b. Insurance companies
   c. Employers
   d. All of the above
3. When you register for medical services, who records your information first?
   a. The doctor
   b. The insurance company
   c. The registration personnel
   d. The nurse
4. Who is responsible for keeping your health information private?
   a. The billing department
   b. The insurance company
   c. You (the patient)
   d. The medical records department
5. To ensure the accuracy of your medical records, you need to make sure that
   a. Your personal information is correct
   b. Your treatment history is accurate and complete
   c. No unfamiliar tests or procedures are recorded
   d. All of the above

Answers:
   1. D   2. D   3. C   4. D   5. B

References

1. "Your personal health information: A guided tour." *myPHR*. 2009. AHIMA. 18 May 2009. http://www.myphr.com/tour/tour_page_01.asp
2. "Notice of privacy practices." *TML IEBP Info*. 2009. TML: Intergovernmental Employee Benefits Pool. 1 Jan 2007. http://www.tmliebp.org/tmliebp/privacy_statement.php
3. "Privacy and security in today's health society." *FierceHealth IT Weekly News for Health IT Leaders*. 2009. FierceHealth. 31 Mar 2009. http://www.fiercehealthit.com/story/privacy-and-secutiry-todays-health-society/2009-03-31
4. "Five things your pharmacist won't tell you." *Health & Well-Being*. 2009. John Tesh: Intelligence for Your Life. 18 May 2009. http://www.tesh.com/ittrium/visit?path=A1x97x1y1xa5x1x76y1x241fx1x9by1x2424x1y5x1bcbfx5x1

Chapter 12

PHP Instructor Materials: Your Personal Health Finances

So you think that money is the root of all evil. Have you ever asked what the root of all money is?

Ayn Rand
Russian-born writer and novelist, 1905–1982

Learning Objectives

1. Introduce concepts of personal healthcare finance
2. Recognize how to manage healthcare bills and validate them
3. Learn how to avoid fraud and medical identity theft
4. Introduce examples of market resources
5. Understand the use of several healthcare forms: Explanation of Benefits and claim history form; healthcare provider account review form

Always Follow the Money: Medical Expenses as Part of the Financial Picture

Managing medical expenses is just as important as managing health information. If it is not done, it is a virtual guarantee that some money will simply disappear. To minimize this risk, start by collecting all financial documents related to current healthcare expenditures. Keep them together as you receive them. This way, you will have them on hand when you are ready to add them to your financial portfolio.

The next few paragraphs explain the importance of keeping all finances up to date, should a healthcare crisis occur.

Patient Instruction Example: What to Do Financially When You Have a Healthcare Crisis; Plan and Save for a Healthcare Crisis; Organize Your Financial Portfolio

A patient recently expressed, "I wish I had a resource to go to that could help me protect my assets while I am dealing with this healthcare crisis." The time to prepare for any financial crisis is now, and your best bet is to initiate a plan prior to the event. The scope of this chapter is about navigating the healthcare system and addressing financial issues in that context. The role of the patient advocate is not about providing financial advice in managing assets. The role is to simply raise questions and suggest the consideration of a professional financial advisor to help manage investments. This book discusses how managing health and managing finances is quite similar—they both progress concurrently in your life.

The following is a sample list of items to consider when searching for a financial advisor:

■ Is the individual a financial advisor, investment advisor, or both?

If an investment advisor, is the individual registered with the Securities and Exchange Commission?

■ Does the advisor have any credentials such as CFP (Certified Financial Planner) or CFA (Chartered Financial Analyst)? (It should be noted, however, that there is no state or federal law requiring those credentials.)
■ Look at credentials and education, and verify if possible. Ask yourself, "Do the credentials and education match the services they are providing?"
■ See if there are any complaints that have been filed with professional boards.
■ Get a list of references and check them (includes bankers, attorneys, and CPAs [certified public accountants]).
■ How long has the advisor been in business?

If unincorporated, check the Secretary of State's office to see how long.

■ Call the County Court Clerk's Office and search for any litigation filed against the advisor. The information may be available online.
■ Check the County Clerk's office to see if there are any judgments filed against the advisor's property. You can do this online through a grantor/grantee search in most counties.
■ Look to see if they have any insurance coverage to protect you, errors and omissions, malpractice, etc.
■ Other questions to ask may include*

---

* SEC.gov

- What experience do you have, especially with people in my circumstances?
- Where did you go to school?
- What is your recent employment history?
- What licenses do you hold? Are you registered with the SEC, a state, or the National Association of Securities Dealers (NASD)?
- What products and services do you offer?
- How are you paid for your services? What is your usual hourly rate, flat fee, or commission?
- Have you ever been disciplined by any government regulator for unethical or improper conduct or sued by a client who was not happy with the work you did?

Other considerations in organizing your financial portfolio may include a general family organizer that addresses the location of several key documents. The following sample is taken from "Collecting and Organizing Your Financial Data" by WINTRUST Wealth Management, which is a document keeper and locator packet.* As with all other sensitive information, please keep these data in a safe place.

PERSONAL INFORMATION

- ■ **Personal Information: You**
  - Your
    - Legal name
    - Date of birth
    - Social security number
    - Legal address
    - Phone numbers: Home, work, and cell
    - Place of birth
    - Organ donor: Yes, no, or undecided
  - Medical care
    - Primary care physician name, address, and phone number
    - Health insurance plan name and identification number
    - Medicare, Medigap, or Medicaid number
    - Blood type
    - Allergies
    - Medications and dosages
    - Dentist name, address, and phone number
  - Employer
    - Name, address, and phone number
    - Human resources contact name and number
    - Supervisor name and number
  - Additional notes

---

* "Collecting and Organizing Your Financial Data" www.wintrust.com

■ **Personal Information: Your Spouse**
  – Your spouse
    • Legal name
    • Date of birth
    • Social security number
    • Legal address
    • Phone numbers: Home, work, and cell
    • Place of birth
    • Organ donor: Yes, no, or undecided
  – Medical care
    • Primary care physician name, address, and phone number
    • Health insurance plan name and identification number
    • Medicare, Medigap, or Medicaid number
    • Blood type
    • Allergies
    • Medications and dosages
    • Dentist name, address, and phone number
  – Employer
    • Name, address, and phone number
    • Human resources contact name and number
    • Supervisor name and number
  – Additional notes
■ **Contacts**
  – Emergency contacts
    • List name, relationship, address, e-mail, and numbers (home, cell, and work)
  – Family
    • List name, relationship, social security number, address if not living with you, e-mail, and numbers (home, cell, and work)
  – Guardian, caretaker, personal representative, or successor trustee
    • List name, role, address, e-mail, and numbers (home, cell, and work)
  – Professional contacts (financial advisor, attorney, accountant, etc.)
    • List name, role, address, e-mail and numbers (home, cell, and work)
  – Household contacts
    • Heating/air conditioning
  – List name, account number, address, e-mail, and numbers (home, cell, and work) associated with the account
    • Home security
  – List name, account number, address, e-mail, and numbers (home, cell, and work) associated with the account
    • Cable
  – List name, account number, address, e-mail, and numbers (home, cell, and work) associated with the account
    • Electrician

- List name, account number, address, e-mail, and numbers (home, cell, and work) associated with the account
  - Plumbing
- List name, account number, address, e-mail, and numbers (home, cell, and work) associated with the account
- Other contacts
  - Type of contact
    - List name, account number, role, address, e-mail, and numbers (home, cell, and work) associated with the account

DOCUMENTS

- Identification (note location and additional details for each)
  - Social security card
  - Birth certification
  - Passport
  - Employment records
  - Military papers
  - Citizenship papers
- Health and family (note location and additional details for each)
  - Health records
  - Marriage certificate
  - Divorce/separation documents
  - Prenuptial agreement
  - Adoption papers
- Finances (note date, location, and additional details for each)
  - Will
  - Spouse's will
  - Durable power of attorney
  - Healthcare directive
  - Living will
  - Trust(s)
  - Tax returns
  - Mortgage documents
  - Bank statements
  - Investment statements
  - Credit card statements
  - Insurance policies
- Property (note property type, location, and additional details)
  - Real estate titles or deeds
  - Vehicle title(s)
  - Appraisals

ACCOUNTS

- Investment and retirement accounts
  - List for each the name of the institution, contact, type, account title, account number, and beneficiary(ies)
- Annuities
  - List for each annuity the owner, type, issuer, contact, insured, beneficiary(ies), and death benefit
- Bank accounts
  - List for each the name of the institution, contact, type, account title, account number, and beneficiary(ies)
- Education savings accounts
  - List for each the issuer, contact, account type, account number, and beneficiary(ies)
- Trust accounts
  - List for each the name of the institution, address, type of trust, tax identification number, current trustee(s), successor trustee(s), and beneficiary(ies)
- Loan and credit card accounts
  - List for each the institution, issuer, type, account number, and contact
- Life insurance
  - List for each the owner, type, issuer, contact, insured, beneficiary(ies), and death benefit
- Health and long-term care insurance
  - List for each the policy type, policy owner, issuer, account number, contact, and coverage amount
- Property
  - List for each the policy type, policy owner, issuer, account number, contact, and contract coverage amount

PERSONAL PROPERTY

- Real estate
  - List the name and location of each property
- Vehicles
  - List for each the make/model, vehicle identification number (VIN), title, and location
- Valuables
  - List for each the type of property and the location
- Safe deposit box
  - List for each the location of the box, location of keys, authorized parties, and contents

ELECTRONIC ACCOUNT MANAGEMENT

- **Online access**
  - List for each the account number, username, and password
  - If you keep passwords in a separation location, document the location
- **Automatic bill payment**
  - List each account number, payment method, and amount

FUNERAL ARRANGEMENTS

- **Instructions for survivors**
  - List religious affiliation, place of worship, clergy to contact, and phone number
  - Indicate preferences: Burial, cremation, donate body to science, funeral service, memorial service, visitation, open casket, closed casket, flowers, and memorial in lieu of flowers
- **Funeral service**
  - List funeral home, phone number, and address
  - Prepaid funeral expense? If yes, location of title/deed
  - Cemetery location and plot address
  - Flower preference
  - Preferred charity(ies)
  - Music
  - Reading
  - Favorite poems/essays
  - Requested participants
  - If cremation, "I would like my ashes to be handled as follows …"
- **Obituary and death notice information**
  - Decide what type of information to list, such as education, military service, affiliations, employment, honors, awards, and list of survivors.

ADDITIONAL NOTES

In an earlier section of this book, the story of Doug was presented, showing how using the knowledge of Current Procedural Terminology (CPT) codes reversed a denial for a lifesaving procedure. The story continues on adverse events that occurred with his personal finances, insurance coverage pertaining to his disability, and his overall paperwork. Doug requested a disability application from human resources. He was told that he did not need to worry about it because his employer would cover his time off for treatment. Upon returning to work from his treatment regimen, he was let go from his position as part of a company downsizing effort by the organization. This resulted in a sudden loss of income, including the loss of his disability benefits. Doug was directed by his patient advocate to seek out his financial advisor to help him organize all of his assets and ensure that his paperwork was in order, as well as develop a plan to manage day-to-day expenses and preserve his assets.

In addressing the disability issue, Doug maintained detailed employer records. Fortunately, he kept the e-mail in which he requested an application for his disability benefits while he was an employee. Doug's advocate assisted in writing an appeal to his employer and the carrier for not allowing him to execute his right under the disability coverage plan. This denial was overturned and Doug was able to obtain the benefits he had originally paid for and planned in case of an adverse event. Again, this book focuses on managing your ongoing health; however, managing your finances is key, regardless of your health status. It is never too late to start, but it is important to do it now.

Patient Instruction Example: Health Insurance Benefits

Collect all of your Explanation of Benefits forms (EOBs) to manage your health insurance benefits. (EOBs are also sometimes called Explanation of Reviews [EORs].)

Your EOB is what you receive from your insurance company (health plan) every time it receives a claim on your behalf. A claim is what a doctor or hospital submits to your insurance company to be reimbursed for services they provide to you. An EOB shows the benefit determination that your insurance company has made based on the contract it has with your plan sponsor and doctor. Your plan sponsor is typically your employer, a third party benefit program, an independent policy that you purchased, or the government. Typically, you share the cost of your insurance with your plan sponsor. A benefit determination defines who will pay for the claim. It also defines how much money each party expected to pay.

It is important to save your EOBs and regularly review them to ensure that each piece of information is accurate. Check your EOB to make sure that the claim lists the diagnosis that you received on the date that you actually visited your doctor. Specifically, check the following:

- Your name or your dependent's name
- Your social security or member identification number on your insurance card
- Date of visit
- Diagnosis (the ICD code assigned by the provider)
- Procedure(s) (the CPT code assigned by the provider)
- Doctor and/or facility name

If the EOB that you received does not provide all of this information, such as the actual CPT code billed, then request this information from your doctor or care facility.

Also important: If you do not have health insurance through your employer, you must give great care and attention to detail when shopping for a policy for which *you* will pay.

Essential:

- Read the fine print before signing up for a health insurance plan.
- Review coverage exclusions or "hidden" fees that will cause your healthcare coverage costs to increase.
- If you have a pre-existing condition, ask your provider how changes to the benefit plan will be impacted. For example, how much will your chronic condition medication cost? Does the plan cover your specific medication? You may want to use a patient advocate to help you understand the impact of switching from one plan to another.
- If you are not sure about the insurance plan or company that you are reviewing, contact the department of insurance for your state and simply ask, "Is this insurance company registered with the State?" This is the best way to make sure you are not buying fake insurance.

Insurance Checklist:

- Ask for a copy of the plan document: Specifically, a list of any services that are excluded. Also ask for a web site on which the insurer updates what they include and don't include in their coverage.
- Ask for samples of how co-pays are calculated.
- Ask for a specific booklet and website address that defines who is in network and who is considered out of network.
- Clarify if any services have limits of type, quantity or length of treatment.
- Stay vigilant in collecting and reviewing your bills as you receive your services.

Remember: A bad decision can cost you thousands of dollars.

The Importance of Accuracy

To better understand the importance of reviewing your EOBs, here's a real-life case scenario:

> Ashley contacted her advocate with an EOB she had a question about. The EOB listed a $300 claim for a diagnosis of "dry eyes" from her eye doctor. The claim listed the service date as the date on which she had picked up new prescription glasses from her eye doctor. However, neither an office visit nor an exam on that day was included in the EOB. Her insurance company paid the claim. The diagnosis of "dry eyes" went into her medical record. Although she had never made a co-payment, the damage was already done. Her

eye doctor submitted a false claim by fabricating a false diagnosis to get more money and her employer paid for a service she never received. Moreover, the false diagnosis had become part of her permanent medical record. We informed her insurance company and corrected her health record.

Lesson Learned: If you receive a statement for health services or items not rendered, call your insurance company right away. Also call your insurance company if an EOB contains incorrect information. Many insurance companies have a hotline for such concerns. At a minimum, ask to speak to a claims representative. Ask your insurance company to add a note to your file describing the error that you found and continue to follow up with them until the issue has been resolved. Also see Appendix C for a sample form for filing such a request.

Document the name of the person(s) you spoke with and the date. Also ask for a transaction and/or a follow-up number. Follow up all phone calls in writing and send your correspondence by mail, fax, or e-mail. Keep a record of phone calls and copies of the letters you send and receive. This documentation helps ensure that your insurance company or anyone else does not take advantage of you.

If you have secondary health insurance policies, keep those documents separate from your primary health insurance documents.

Impact on Future Insurance Coverage

Submitted claims become part of the claim history that your insurance company keeps about you. Your claim history and any diagnosis submitted by your provider can thus impact the cost of your future health, disability, and life insurance coverage. It is similar to how a false item in your credit report can affect your ability to get a loan. This is yet another reason to carefully scrutinize your EOBs on a regular basis.

Contact your insurance company and ask if your claim history is available online. If not, request a copy of your claim history from your insurance company at least once a year. Your claim history should list all of the claims your insurance company has paid or received on your behalf. Check this list just as you would your EOBs.

Patient Message: Make sure your claim information only contains monies associated with the services you actually received.

Disputing Healthcare Bills

Healthcare billing disputes can occur at two levels. The first is a dispute with your healthcare provider. If you get a bill for services that you never received, contact your provider and request an explanation of the charges. If you still disagree, put your objection in writing to the doctor. Contact your insurance company and let them know of your dispute.

The second level of billing disputes can be with your insurance company. If you receive a statement from your insurance company denying payment for services that have been determined to be medically unnecessary, ask the insurer for a written explanation. A medically unnecessary service or item is anything that is considered not needed for the diagnosis or treatment of your condition. Contact your provider for an explanation, including the medical reason for the service.

If you cannot resolve this between your doctor and insurance company, you can contact the department of insurance for your State to request an appeal.

Patient Message: Don't be shy. Defend yourself and make sure you understand the basis for any explanation provided to you.

Patient Instruction Example: Avoiding Fraud and Medical Identity Theft

The problem of billing errors is often directly related to an incident of medical identity theft or healthcare fraud. By retrieving and reviewing the documents discussed earlier, you can monitor for false claim activity. You can also monitor your insurance company to make sure that they are paying your (and *only* your) claims. As discussed previously, failing to do so and ending up with false claims on your healthcare insurance records can seriously jeopardize your financial health, rendering it difficult or impossible to obtain affordable insurance coverage. And you certainly do not want false claims going toward your benefit coverage cap. (Your benefit coverage cap is the total amount of money your insurance company will pay toward your healthcare claims. Once you exceed your lifetime cap, your policy will no longer cover you).

Again, this problem can usually be resolved by regularly monitoring EOBs and resolving any inaccuracies with your provider or insurer as soon as possible.

Healthcare fraud and medical identity theft can result in

- Being subjected to unsafe or unnecessary medical procedures
- Medical records being compromised
- Insurance information being used to submit false claims
- Ineffective, unsafe drugs/remedies being prescribed
- Unproven treatments/supplements being prescribed
- Fraudulent diagnostic tests (not approved by the Food and Drug Administration [FDA]) being utilized
- Loss of benefit days and capping of insurance benefits

With your detailed and up-to-date Personal Healthcare Portfolio (PHP), you can protect and better advocate for yourself. You will easily be able to access and provide the information required for a patient advocate to help you.

Patient Message: Healthcare costs are out of control, so guard your health and financial information.

Tips for avoiding healthcare fraud*:

■ Never sign blank insurance forms.
■ Never give blanket authorization to a medical provider to bill for services rendered.
■ Ask your medical providers what they will charge and what you will be expected to pay out of pocket.
■ Carefully review your insurer's explanation of the benefits statement. Call your insurer and/or provider if you have questions.
■ Do not do business with door-to-door/telephone salespeople who tell you that services of medical equipment are free.
■ Give your insurance/Medicare identification only to those people who have provided you with medical services.
■ Keep accurate records of all healthcare appointments.
■ Know if your physician has ordered equipment for you.

Patient Instruction Example: I Don't Have Insurance, I Can't Afford It, and I Refuse to Buy It

If you do not have health insurance, you may still have options when deciding how to pay your healthcare bills. If you have been a patient of a major medical facility, contact the patient financial services department. Ask whether they can help you find subsidy programs that may be available to you. Ask a patient advocate to work with you in helping navigate options under the current Affordable Care Act or any other emerging program. You can also contact your state to ask whether you qualify for publicly available resources. You can also contact a patient advocate who will help you find the right program or payment option for you. Finally, if you do not qualify for any assistance, ask your provider if they have a sliding scale based on income for patients and payment plan options.

Patient Message: Do not be afraid to ask for help.

Sample Health Information Request Forms

This section includes the following sample forms, based on forms used by Medical Business Associates' patient advocates, to request (1) copies of patient EOBs and claim histories from insurance companies and (2) a review of patient accounts from healthcare providers.

---

* www.fbi.gov/scams-safety/fraud

APPENDIX 12.1: EXPLANATION OF BENEFITS AND CLAIM HISTORY FORM

[Date]

To: [Insurance Company Name
        Insurance Company Address]

Re: [Patient Name
        Date of Birth
        Social Security Number or Member ID
        Group Number]

Dear [Insurance Company Name],

Enclosed please find a release of information and consent from the above patient.

Please provide the following information:

_____ A complete list of EOBs (Explanation of Benefits) listing all claims submitted under the social security number and employer group number given above

_____ If available, the actual facility and professional bill submitted

_____ Any medical records that have been provided to you

_____ Any electronic records that are not maintained in hard-copy form

Please forward your information to [your address].

Please feel free to contact me at [your contact information].

Sincerely,

[Your name]

APPENDIX 12.2: HEALTHCARE PROVIDER ACCOUNT REVIEW FORM

[Date]
[Institution Name]
[Institution Address]
[Institution City, State, ZIP]
[CFO Name]
Re: [Patient Name], Account [Patient Account Number], Date Admitted
        [Admittance Date]
Dear Mr./Ms. [Director of Patient Financial Services],
I am writing to request your full and thorough review of my account. I received your balance due notice indicating that I owe $[Amount Due] on the account. Please be advised that I do not believe the charges reflect the services rendered. I am exercising my rights under HIPAA and the Fair Credit & Collection Act to verify these charges. Please accept this letter as my consent to release a copy of the itemized bill, UB-92, UB-04, CMS-1450, and/or CMS-1500. Within these forms, I would like a listing of all diagnosis codes and procedure codes within 30 days of receipt of this letter. If my bill is being processed with a payment methodology that does not include itemized charges, please provide the basis such as a DRG group, APG, RUG group, and so forth. Please forward a copy of any financial responsibility agreement contained within my file.
The requested information should be sent to my attention at the address below. I will pay for any reasonable copy cost associated with this request. Thank you for your prompt assistance with this matter.
Sincerely,
[Your name]
[Address]
[Contact Number]

Study Questions

1. Who is someone you should hire to help manage your assets?
   a. Paralegal
   b. Life coach
   c. Financial advisor
   d. Psychologist
2. Which of the following would you NOT include in your financial portfolio?
   a. Employment information
   b. Lines of credit
   c. Contact information
   d. School transcripts
3. Your (_____) is what you receive from your insurance company every time it receives a claim on your behalf.
   a. EOB
   b. Plan review
   c. Progress report
   d. None of the above
4. A (_____) defines who will pay for the claim.
   a. Plan sponsor
   b. Physician
   c. Adjuster
   d. Benefit determination
5. You should check your EOB for which of the following?
   a. Date of visit
   b. Your name or dependent's name
   c. Services rendered to you
   d. All of the above

Answer Key:
   1. C   2. D   3. A   4. D   5. D

Chapter 13

PHP Instructor Materials: Protecting Your PHP in a Buyer-Beware Market

If it had been possible to build the Tower of Babel without climbing it, it would have been permitted.

Franz Kafka
Austrian poet, 1883–1924

Learning Objectives

1. Recognize the dynamics of a buyer-beware market
2. Learn how to protect yourself and your Personal Healthcare Portfolio (PHP)
3. Understand how to safeguard your Protected Health Information (PHI)
4. Identify the red flags of healthcare fraud and medical errors
5. Be aware of the life-changing events that may impact your ability to manage your healthcare

This chapter is dedicated to materials on protecting PHP information and buyer-beware concepts that should be considered when working with individuals as an advocate.

Patient Instruction Example: Protect Yourself

Chapter 2 discussed how the patient has a bigger stake in controlling and managing his or her care. Greater patient involvement comes with more responsibility to be vigilant in monitoring all data related to healthcare needs. Furthermore, in the environment of the Internet of Things, consumers can have instant communication and transactions with an increasing number of virtual strangers. Access has its privileges to creative software as a service (SaaS) program in providing value to consumers. However, vulnerabilities in encountering other individuals or organizations that are ethically challenged, and at times dangerous, are higher than ever. Healthcare has become increasingly complicated and fragmented with new terminology that is not understood by the average consumer. The fragmented market, a market with rapid and ongoing change, is ripe for fraud, waste, and abuse. The patient advocate should include a discussion on the "stranger danger" rules of healthcare. It is important to warn consumers about signs and symptoms of fraud, waste, and abuse that exist within this complex marketplace. This chapter will include examples of the theme of "buyer beware." In a buyer-beware environment, it is important to understand the flow of money. In the private sector, the flow of money begins when the patient seeks a healthcare service:

- The patient needs/gets healthcare services
- The provider performing the service wants to get paid
- The payer wants to manage their risk and make sure they collect more premiums than claims paid out.
- The plan sponsor (typically the employer) wants to offer defined program benefits at an economical cost.

In contrast, the public sector has a plan sponsor for programs like Medicare and Medicaid. They focus on attributes similar to the private sector with respect to stakeholders. However, the provision of health services is at a legislated set price. The plan driver tends to be the political structure and the taxpayer who is funding the public program.

The Bottom Line: Government-sponsored programs tend to have layered incentives that go beyond simply health. In the private sector, the point of interest is on profit margins from increased revenues and/or reducing costs. In contrast, the public sector may provide conflicting messages because power, influence, and control are imbedded within the process.

Example of Monetary Incentives: An insurance company makes money when it pays for fewer services. A provider makes money when it provides *more* services. Such conflicts exist throughout the healthcare system. So, who is in the middle? A large and growing army of criminals, and they don't discriminate. They will steal from the insurance company, the patient, or the provider.

Healthcare is an enormous industry and is only expected to get bigger. In 1902, healthcare expenditures were 25% of gross domestic product (GDP).* U.S.

---

* http://www.usgovernmentspending.com/healthcare_spending

healthcare spending grew 5.3% in 2014, reaching $3.0 trillion or $9523 per person. As a share of the nation's GDP, health spending accounted for 17.5%.*

Trillions of dollars are being exchanged through the fragmented and complicated healthcare delivery channels. The high volume high transaction market makes it ripe for FWA. As a consumer on the front line, you are in the best position to protect yourself from being a victim of healthcare fraud.

Mismanagement of healthcare information and outright fraud hurts people. It causes disability, financial devastation, and, in some cases, death. It can affect your health, home, family, assets, and community. Healthcare fraud[1] comes in many different forms, including (but not limited to):

- Medical identity theft
- Illegal prescription drug sales
- Adulterated and counterfeit prescription drugs
- Medically unnecessary healthcare services
- Patient neglect and abuse
- Patient experimentation
- False healthcare claim submittal

Consider carefully the following guidelines as you manage your healthcare actions and experiences, and remember one simple, important rule: If something does not seem right, listen to your gut. Get a second opinion from a patient advocate or someone else you trust. For more information about healthcare fraud and for special alerts, visit the Center for Medicaid and Medicare Services Web site (www.cms.gov). Ethically challenged people lurk in all types of settings. Healthcare is no exception.

Patient Message: In addition to the countless bureaucratic and process-related traps to avoid, there is a growing risk of being victimized by fraudsters. The best protection is information. So please, educate yourself.

Healthcare Provider Fraud and Errors

Invalid Licenses: Some doctors practice without a valid license. Sometimes they continue to practice with an expired license or with a suspended license. Sometimes they never received a license in the first place. Most states have an online department of professional regulation. Use the Internet to find the department of professional regulation for your state, and look up your provider to make sure they have an active license. In fact, most online programs will even disclose whether the provider ever had a disciplinary action against them.

---

* https://www.cms.gov/research-statistics-data-and-systems/statistics-trends-and-reports/nationalhealthexpenddata/nationalhealthaccountshistorical.html

Bad and Low-Quality Healthcare or Outright Quackery: Believe it, because it happens. Unqualified and untrained surgeons perform surgeries. Doctors use defective medical equipment to perform exams. Pharmacists dispense adulterated and expired drugs. Doctors perform expensive and life-threatening treatments that patients do not need. The list goes on. Check the reputation of your doctors and facilities and look for complaints lodged against them. One resource for these types of background checks, again, is your state department of professional regulation or local Better Business Bureau. You can also check public records for filed legal actions.

Medication Delivery Errors and Fraud: Hospitals in the United States cause deaths each year because patients are given the wrong prescriptions at the wrong time with the wrong dosages. In some cases, patients do not receive their medications at all. Make sure that you understand your medication regimen and that the hospital staff is adhering to it.

Phantom Treatments: Some healthcare criminals bill insurance companies for services that were never received by patients. If you receive a bill that does not make sense, call your insurance company.

Patient Message: If you are told you need a treatment that does not make sense to you, get a second opinion.

Double Billing: Unethical doctors or third-party billing companies may double or triple bill health insurance companies for the same treatments. Their hope is that the insurance companies will not discover these fraudulent duplicate claims. When they don't, the results are overpayments by insurance companies, extra co-pays for patients, and the usage of patients' lifetime cap coverage or maximum allowable treatment volumes amounts. You should always review any explanation of benefits (EOB) that you receive and ask yourself, "Did I actually see that doctor and receive those services?" If the answer is no, call your insurance company immediately.

Patient Message: Speak to your provider, specifically your doctor. Sometimes, an agent of the doctor is the cause of the problem and your doctor may not even be aware that his or her billing company is filing false claims.

Medical Identity Theft and Fraud: Fraudsters can cause a lot of problems when they get their hands on a patient's personal health information and identity. *Examples*:

- Stealing a patient's insurance card to obtain healthcare services for themselves
- Using a patient's health insurance card to submit false claims and generate bills for services that the patient never received

Problem: If you don't monitor your EOBs, your credit score can be affected by unpaid healthcare bills. It is also possible for perpetrators to generate medical records under another patient's name. This can not only cause financial harm but can put your health and possibly your life in jeopardy. For example, you could be on the operating table and receive the wrong blood type because fraudulent healthcare records created as a result of using your identity attributed to you contain information about someone else.

Rolling Labs: Beware of rolling motor vans and mobile facilities that show up at local malls and public places. They often provide services like free screenings or exams. Deals too good to be true often are just that. Scammers often provide needless services and bill for tests and exams never performed. Sometimes, they're just out to steal your personal information. Never give out your personal information for these types of free screenings. Visit reputable doctors and clinics for *all* of your healthcare needs.

Misleading Contracts: Does "buy now and pay later" sound familiar to you? If a doctor forces you to sign a contract for discounted services, make sure to read the fine print. The contract may obligate you to pay, even if you stop receiving services, without any recourse.

Fraudulent Consent Forms: Legitimate consent forms typically explain medical procedures and treatments and allow your doctors to share information with other healthcare professionals. Get a second opinion if any consent form has contractual language that waives any of your patient rights or overrides any contract with your insurance company.

Patient Message: There are countless ways to be victimized by healthcare fraudsters. Be an alert consumer.

Pharmacy Fraud and Errors

Prescription Mix-Ups[2]: Mistakes with medication occur more often than you think. In fact, thousands of errors are made every day across the country. One hospital on the East Coast mixed up medication for roughly one in eight prescriptions filled.

Self-Defense: Take an active role in your care. Check your pills to ensure that you have been given the drug that your doctor prescribed and read prescription labels before leaving the pharmacy. Many drugs have similar names, which can cause confusion. Misfiled prescriptions can be deadly or result in severe injuries. If you have questions about your prescription, ask your pharmacist or doctor. Frequently asked questions include

- What is this medication for?
- How long do I take this prescription?
- Can this medication interfere with any other prescription or over-the-counter medication that I am currently taking?
- What if I miss a dose?

"Partial-Fills": These occur when a pharmacy only partially fills a prescription and you are billed for the entire amount. If you believe that you have received a partial prescription, contact your pharmacy immediately and return for the remainder of the prescription.[3] One of my patients ran out of her child's Adderall prior to the prescribed 30 days. She (Mom) reported it to her pharmacy immediately. The pharmacy told her they filled it completely and reported her to law enforcement because, from their perspective, the mother must have lost the missing 30 days. On her next prescription refill, she checked her medications and counted the pills in front of the pharmacist. It was wrong again. This time she contacted the hotline for the pharmacy chain and reported the error.

Overworked Pharmacists: Your pharmacists will not tell you when they are overworked. This issue can be found in both rural and populated areas. For example, a rural area heavily populated with the elderly may require more staff time. In comparison, a big city environment may have issues with just high volume. Pharmacists typically have less than 5 minutes to input your prescription, print the label, count out the pills, and counsel you on proper dosage and side effects. You must ensure that the pharmacist gives you the drug you were actually prescribed and that the pills in your bottle are the right ones. You can also use website resources such as www.drugs.com to verify the accuracy of the color and shape of the pills prescribed.* The most current reliable source for looking up details, pictures, and notices of a specific medication is www.fda.gov.

Generic versus Brand: Swapping generic drugs for brand names (or a similar drug from another manufacturer) is not a common problem but when it does occur, it can be dangerous—especially if you are taking thyroid, heart, or epilepsy medications. Pharmacists can make these types of swaps without your permission. Make sure to request that your pharmacists place a note in your file so that they cannot swap brands without consulting your doctor.†

Patient Message: Learn to look at your medications, look up pictures at www.fda.gov, and monitor and keep a diary for any changes in how the medication affects you.

Insurance Company (Payer) Fraud and Errors

Fake Insurance: Dishonest insurance agents and brokers sell discount cards and insurance cards for fake policies. Any health insurance plans that are priced below industry norms or are being sold as a limited time offer are likely to be fake. False insurance plans can leave patients in a compromising situation, especially when they are sick. Becoming suddenly ill and needing medical care is *not* the time you want to learn that your premium payments were not providing you coverage. Before purchasing healthcare insurance, check with your state's insurance department to find out if the insurance agent or broker is licensed and if the insurance company they represent is registered with the state. If your doctors are trying to collect from you because your insurance company will not pay,

---

* "Five Things Your Pharmacist Won't Tell You."
† Ibid.

immediately pick up the phone and call your insurance company and request all explanations in writing. If they do not cooperate, contact a patient advocate, state department of insurance or your attorney.

Bad Faith: When an insurance company denies a legitimate claim without cause, contact your state's insurance program or a patient advocate for support. Make sure that you follow up with your insurance company and obtain in writing the reason why a service or product is not being covered. Make sure to follow all the procedures to properly appeal your request for coverage.

Patient Message: Every state has its own department of insurance. Your state's department of insurance may be found online by simply searching for "(your state) department of insurance." If you are not satisfied with the results (from your insurance plan) of the appeal process, request the procedure from your insurance company on how to submit your appeal to your state department of insurance.

Drug and Medical Equipment Supplier Fraud and Errors

Internet Savings: Buying medications from an unknown source can result in drugs and medical equipment that are counterfeit, adulterated, stored improperly, or contaminated. Getting a prescription from a doctor who conducts physicals over the phone is an obvious recipe for disaster. Just like seeing reputable doctors, getting your drugs and medical equipment from trusted sources minimizes your exposure to fraud. If your benefit plan has an online pharmacy, make sure that when you do go to your benefit plan's website you look up at the top to ensure that the page did not direct you to a fraudulent web address. For example, if you go to www.mbaaudit.com, look at the Uniform Resource Locator (URL) and make sure you were not redirected to a different address. Fraudsters will mimic legitimate companies and try to sabotage their websites by luring unsuspecting patients to a fraudulent site to collect personal details, credit card data, and other information later used to commit identity fraud.

Counterfeit and Adulterated Drugs: Perpetrators actually make counterfeit medications out of almost any substance that they can get their hands on. Some substances do not cause harm to patients but some, such as pesticides in powder form, can cause irreparable damage.

Self-Defense:

■ If you take medication for a long-term illness, save the packaging that your prescription is dispensed in. When you refill your prescription, compare the new packaging with the old. If you notice any difference (no matter how minor) such as changes in the lettering or font changes in the numbers or shapes, return the package immediately for verification.

■ If you receive pills in a vial that is not packaged, look at the pill itself. You can always go to www.fda.gov and find a picture of the drug and compare it with what you have in your hand. If something does not look right or the packaging appears to have been tampered with or damaged, return the drug to your pharmacy.

■ Search for fraudulent activity associated with your specific drug using the Food and Drug Administration (FDA) web site (www.fda.gov). The FDA will publish notices of found counterfeit medications.

■ If you are taking a medication and it just does not feel like it works the way it normally does—take a closer look at it and contact your doctor immediately.

"Crossing the Border": Counterfeit drugs are a huge problem around the globe. In some countries, the rate at which counterfeit drugs is dispensed is as high as 50% of total prescriptions filled.[4]

Self-Defense: Closely examine old or damaged-looking containers as well as labels that appear to show any signs of print deviations. Buying medications in the United States is not necessarily the answer. The data in the United States are not clear; however, estimates indicate that between 1% and 10% of prescription drugs sold in the United States are counterfeit or adulterated. Take the time to learn about your medications. Your health and livelihood could be on the line.

Patient Message: Buyers beware—do your homework because sometimes you get what you pay for.

Divorce Behaviors

It's not always an unfamiliar face that can cripple your PHP. With some 50% of marriages ending in divorce, a discussion of the consequences of divorce and how it affects families is a must in any advocacy book. Marital or other family disputes can interrupt the family's healthcare schematic, causing confusion, financial hardship, and potential health disasters. Healthcare is not normally a priority focus in divorce, but it should be.

This point was brought home in the following patient scenario:

A practicing nurse in a medical intensive care unit (MICU) is taking care of a 16-year-old male patient within the adult MICU. The patient has advanced cardiomyopathy. This condition occurs when the heart muscle is swollen and inflamed. It prevents the heart from working as it should. The condition is typically seen more in adults over the age of 70, not 16. The doctors could not determine why he had it. Was it viral? Was it drug abuse? He was subjected to a series of ongoing tests and psychological analyses.

During conversations with the patient, he started to talk about his family. He mentioned that his parents were divorced. When asked for how long, he stated four years. As the conversation progressed, he was asked about his orthodontic braces. "How long have you had your braces?" asked his nurse. He replied, "Four years." The nurse followed up with, "When was the last time you checked in with your orthodontists?" Again, his response was, "Four years."

A STAT (immediate attention) consult for an orthodontist was ordered in the MICU. The result of the exam was that an infection starting at the back of the patient's mouth had grown and progressed like a tunnel (fistula) to his heart. His lack of regular visits to the orthodontist resulted in a serious medical condition that, in essence, compromised his heart for the remainder of his life.

Lesson Learned: When it comes to healthcare, we as individuals can be our own worst enemies. It is a complicated market and should not be intertwined with marital or other family disputes. Payment for the patient's orthodontia was in dispute between his divorced mother and father and was stuck in a court system that would not make a decision on accountability. *Here are a few other case studies of divorce versus family healthcare:*

- A divorce agreement stipulates that the father is to provide health insurance. Unbeknownst to the mother, the father failed to follow the court order and canceled the insurance coverage on his children. The mother continued to take the kids to the doctor. The employer never notified the mother of the termination and neglected to offer Consolidated Omnibus Budget Reconciliation Act (COBRA) coverage. The father then started to contact his children's healthcare providers and remove his name as the father and guarantor and place each medical account in the name of his children. The creditors then began pursuing the children for payment. The kids' school system required health exams for all students, but no provider would see the children without insurance.

- A post-decree motion (a motion that occurs after a divorce has been finalized) was issued regarding the payment of the two children's college costs. The motion was one of the most poorly written documents of violating a person's right to privacy that I had ever seen; therefore, I could not even reproduce a redacted copy of it. In essence, a mother disclosed real and false protected health information about both of her children. The premise of the argument was to use their health information as an argument as to why they (the children) did not need a college education and that she should not have to contribute because the education would be a waste of money. In the meantime, the personal health information that is federally protected cannot be removed from the court's filing system. The egregious behavior? The son had learning disabilities and the daughter was suffering from depression; therefore, the mother felt that it was pointless to spend any money on them for college.

- A couple whose divorce was pending were having a dispute. In an act of anger, the wife called 911 and told the police that her husband was contemplating suicide. She reported that he had just taken an overdose of several medications. The husband was restrained and forcibly admitted to a psychiatric institution for a 24-hour observation. All of his blood work came back negative and his system was clear of any medications. Since that time, however, he has had difficulty obtaining health, disability, and life insurance.

■ A divorced couple both remarried. While in the care of his stepmother, the couple's child hit his head against a tree and severely injured his right eye. There was an inch of swelling contained within the eye socket. The stepmother prevented the child from reporting the injury to his mother (who happened to be a healthcare professional). The stepmother covered the eye with a bandage, gave the child Motrin (which increases bleeding), and sent him to school the next day. Needless to say, the child's condition worsened (the school nurse contacted mom) before he received the necessary medical care.

Patient Message: Keep your divorce issues separate from managing your health and that of your children. Open lines of communication are key among children living in multiple households.

Lesson Learned: If any area exists for civil compromise and effective communication, it would be in managing the health of the children involved. Family matters such as divorce, business affairs, and so forth should *not* be played out in managing one's health or left to a series of legal events and delayed motions. This could result in disability, adverse outcomes, and/or even death.

Study Guide

1. An insurance company makes money by paying for (_____) services; which of the following fits best?
   a. More
   b. Fewer
   c. Expensive
   d. None of the above
2. Healthcare fraud can cause
   a. Financial devastation
   b. Death
   c. Disability
   d. All of the above
3. Which of the following is NOT a form of healthcare fraud?
   a. Medical identity theft
   b. Counterfeit drugs
   c. Patient neglect
   d. None of the above
4. A provider makes money when it provides (_____) services.
   a. More
   b. Fewer

  c. Expensive

  d. None of the above

5. "Some healthcare criminals bill insurance companies for services never received by patients." What is this defined as?

  a. Double billing

  b. Phantom billing

  c. Ghost services

  d. None of the above

Answer Key:

  1. B 2. D 3. C 4. A 5. B

References

1. Busch, R. *Healthcare Fraud Auditing and Detection Guide*. Hoboken, NJ: John Wiley, 2008.
2. Jaret, P. Prescription for trouble. *Consumer Health Interactive*. 2009. HealthyMe! 15 Jan 2009.
3. Obgyn.com. CVS pharmacy settles with states over alleged faulty billing practice. *Legal Issues*. 27 Jan 2003. http://www.obygn.net/newsheadlines/headline_medical_news-Legal_Issues-20030127-3.asp
4. Phnom Penh Post. Counterfeit drug trafficking rife in kingdom experts say. http://www.phnompenhpost.com/index.php/2009111929641/National-news/counterfeit-drug-trafficking-rife-in-kingdom-experts-say.html. November 19, 2009.

Chapter 14

PHP Instructor Materials: Creating a Personal Healthcare Portfolio

We must become the change we want to see in the world.

Mahatma Gandhi
Indian philosopher, 1869–1948

Learning Objectives

1. Learn how to develop your own healthcare portfolio.
2. Learn to use your healthcare portfolio.
3. Discover additional healthcare market resources.

This chapter is dedicated to materials on how to prepare a Personal Healthcare Portfolio (PHP) and other relevant concepts that should be considered in working with individuals as an advocate.

Patient Instruction Example

The best time to start your PHP is *now*. Your PHP can be as simple or as comprehensive as you want to make it. Do not wait until you or your family member has a healthcare crisis. However, if you have recently had a crisis, it is not too late. Healthcare issues can take an emotional toll on everyone involved, so it's important to prepare before a crisis occurs. You may be in charge of a loved one or disabled child's care and have to plan for them as well as yourself. The optimal time to assemble your PHP is when you have the time to be thorough and the energy to dedicate yourself to the process. However, using the directions contained in your PHP (Section III), you can start assembling your health information in less than 20 minutes.

Getting Started on Your Personal Healthcare Portfolio

The amount of time and energy needed to maintain your PHP is different for everyone. It will depend on the extent of your healthcare history. It will also depend on whether or not you have specific healthcare needs. Remember that, for your PHP to be most effective, you should update it with each new piece of information related to your healthcare.

Assembling and maintaining your PHP can be time-consuming (and in some cases overwhelming). But your investment will be worthwhile. With your up-to-date PHP, you will be in a much better position to quickly and accurately address your health issues. All of your related information will be organized in one place and readily available to you.

Think of the time and energy that you would spend training for a marathon. Most runners spend between three months and one year preparing and maintaining themselves for one day of running. Without preparation, running a marathon is much more difficult than it would be with the proper training. Similarly, preparing and maintaining your PHP makes it easier for you to navigate our healthcare system, making decisions about your health much less difficult to make.

Patient advocates can be helpful in assembling and maintaining your PHP. To get started on your PHP, *follow three easy steps*:

1. Schedule 20 minutes to start your PHP.
2. Take 5 minutes to gather as much information and as many records and materials as you can find right away (e.g., medical records, explanations of benefits [EOBs], insurance information, and other information sources that you think are relevant to your healthcare). Do not worry about finding every piece of information related to your healthcare right now.
3. Fill in your information on the forms in the following sections, as referenced in the appendix (PHP starter kit) (to the best of your ability):
   a. Personal information
   b. Emergency contacts
   c. Health insurance
   d. Healthcare providers
   e. Active (existing) illness
   f. Allergies
   g. Medications (start by only entering the medications that you are currently taking)

If you have more time to devote to creating your PHP, the next sections to fill out are

a. Family history
b. Surgeries
c. Illness history
d. Test results (most recent)

Once you have created your initial PHP patient profile (see sample templates in Section III):

1. You may want to get a binder with tabs that you can use to keep additional documents in an organized fashion, following the outline of your PHP.
2. Collect and record all information and materials that you currently have and/ or know of that are related to your health, wellness, healthcare financials, personal assessments, and documents.
3. Categorize the collected information within the sections provided.
4. Make a list of all the healthcare providers that you have ever seen—including doctors, nurse practitioners, pharmacies, hospitals, physical therapists, chiropractors, home health nurses, personal trainers, massage therapists, etc.
5. Contact each healthcare provider to find out their specific procedure for obtaining copies of your medical records. Hospitals will typically put you in contact with the medical records department or someone who manages the release of patient health information. Each healthcare provider will advise you of their specific policy and procedure for retrieving your information. Review the policy and submit your request. If you ever have difficulties obtaining your information, ask to speak to the provider's compliance officer. You can use the Consent for Release of Information Form in Chapter 2 to submit a request for your medical records.
6. Make a list of your current and previous health insurance companies.
7. Contact each insurance company to ask for a printed history of your records, EOBs, and every bill that was submitted under your name. You can use the EOB and Claim History Form in Chapter 2 to submit requests for your EOBs.
8. If you need or want help from a patient advocate to help you through this process, they are only a phone call away. Make sure they are certified and have the correct training. Trained patient advocates can be a great resource to create and maintain your PHP. They can answer *any* question regarding your healthcare experience or help direct you to someone who can.

Some additional important do's and don'ts about managing your PHP:

1. *Do* ensure that you keep track of every person who you share your PHP with. There is space to do so in the "Health—Basic Info—Shared Log" section.
2. *Do* make a backup copy of your PHP annually. Keep it in a safety deposit box or with someone dependable who you trust. You should also give a

copy of your PHP to the person who is in charge of your advance directives (a signed legal document in which you express your wishes in the event you cannot speak for yourself).

3. *Do* bring your PHP to your medical appointments.

4. *Do* keep your PHP current and update it with each new piece of health information you obtain.

5. *Do* keep copies of your living will and your power of attorney in the appropriate section so that they are easily accessible. Too often, these documents are locked in a bank vault or out of reach when families need them. The most important reason for creating a living will is to let your desires be known when you are unable to advocate for yourself. If you do not make a living will, you potentially place critical decisions about your health in the hands of another party or the legal system.

   a. When drafting your living will and power of attorney, designate two or three trusted individuals—just in case the primary designee is unable to fulfill his or her responsibilities on your behalf. List the different situations where the designation would shift from one person to another. Think through whom you would want to give the responsibility of executing your wishes. Although it is typical to designate a spouse, consider who else might serve as your second or third designee. You could choose an adult child, parent, sibling, or even a close friend if you believe a family member might be too emotionally involved to make rational decisions during a medical emergency.

6. *Do* keep copies and records of any research you do pertaining to your health. Research can help you verify information that you are receiving from your doctors. Your research notes may also come in handy when you are making decisions in the future. If you join support groups or interest groups, keep relevant documents that provide for future reference in the appropriate section.

7. *Do* verify the legitimacy of your healthcare providers. State departments of professional regulation allow you to verify whether a doctor holds a valid license to practice and look up related documented disciplinary or suspension issues. As discussed earlier, people have been known to practice without licenses or to fabricate their degrees altogether.

8. *Do not* leave your original PHP with anyone—no matter who they are. If one of your doctors needs a copy of your information, then make copies for them. Always retain the original information. Your original PHP contains many original documents that may be difficult or impossible to replace.

9. *Do not* include non-health-related items of a personal nature (e.g., your marriage or divorce certificate). All items in your PHP should reflect issues related to your health.

Patient Instruction: Take one step at a time; this will help prevent you from being overwhelmed.

A Personal Healthcare Portfolio in Action

An Example of Preventing a Medical Error

The following is a real example of why maintaining an accurate health history is so important. Remember a prior discussion on patient "Patty," and her experiences with intraoperative awakening? As explained, Patty had undergone surgery and experienced the rare but highly unpleasant syndrome where she could hear and feel the surgery but couldn't communicate with anyone in the operating room. Following this procedure, it was noted in family discussions that her daughter never responded to dental anesthesia. In addition, Patty mentioned that her mother had experienced intraoperative awakening during her heart bypass surgery. In essence, Patty had a known family history of family members NOT responding to anesthesia. The advocate had Patty include the anesthesia report in her PHP. She then required all future anesthesiologists to read her anesthesia report and include in their plan of care provisions in order to not repeat the experience again. The result of Patty taking control of her care? She never experienced intraoperative awakening again in any of her subsequent surgeries.

Key Questions: Did the first anesthesiologist make a medical error? Did this anesthesiologist make choices about Patty's care without adequate information (family history of NON-responsiveness to anesthesia)? We will never know. What we do know is that supplying your doctor with your PHP with a complete family history can help you prevent these sorts of medical complications.

Ongoing Process: Have a Comprehensive Yet Fluid PHP

This book provides a simple way for patients to take control of their healthcare. By collecting the necessary documents and sharing them with doctors, as an advocate you are helping to make sure that the patient receives the best and safest medical care possible.

Patient Instruction Example

When you visit your doctors, make sure that they understand your health history. This way, your doctor can recommend the best options for you and you can make the most informed healthcare decisions. Keep copies of questions that you have asked your doctors, their answers, and any other notes that you take during your office visits. Make sure that you designate people who know your medical wishes, put them in writing, (such as a living will or power attorney for healthcare) and keep copies in your PHP—just in case the worst happens. If you are preparing a PHP for a loved one, identify and document their wishes so that a successor can continue their PHP planning/execution.

Finally, establish a relationship with your health plan (insurance company). Keep the EOBs they send you. Request a claim history annually.

You are in the best position to make sure that no false claims are being submitted on your behalf and to make sure that your health plan (insurance company) is only paying for services that you receive.

Sample Market Resources to Help Prepare Your PHP

Patient advocates are trained to maintain patient privacy according to practice standards, state, and federal laws. If you need assistance getting started on your PHP, have a need or problem beyond your control, or just need to ask an independent party for advice, contact one of the following resources (see Chapter 13 for additional resources):

1. Medical, financial, administrative, and information resources, such as

■ **Medical Business Associates**
www.mbaaudit.com
630.789.9000
E-mail a patient advocate: patientadvocate@mbaaudit.com

Our patient advocates help facilitate an understanding of healthcare. They navigate patients through its complex world, answer patient questions, and help resolve concerns. Healthcare infomediary advocates also help patients assemble, maintain, and use their PHPs. Medical Business Associates provides a tool and the resources to manage medical expenses. We also offer medical identity theft support services for victims of medical errors; financial errors; and fraud, waste, and abuse.

■ **Agency for Healthcare Research and Quality**
www.ahrq.gov
301.427.1364

This federal agency aims to improve the quality, safety, efficiency, and effectiveness of healthcare for all Americans. Their web site includes clinical practice guidelines for both physicians and consumers. The "Consumers and Patients" section provides information on health plans, prescriptions, prevention and wellness, quality of healthcare, questions to ask, smoking, and surgery.2. Disease-specific resources, such as

■ **The American Cancer Society**
www.cancer.org
800.227.2345

Cancer information specialists are available 24/7 to answer questions about specific cancers, treatment options, side effects, coping with cancer, medicines, pain control, clinical trials, prevention, screening, and quitting tobacco. They can refer cancer patients to many local and national resources, including patient services, support groups, social services, medical equipment, wigs and prostheses, transportation, lodging, and financial programs.

■ **American Diabetes Association**

www.diabetes.org

800.342.2383

Representatives guide patients to information on diabetes, as well as programs and events. In addition to offering brochures/pamphlets on a variety of diabetes topics, American Diabetes Association representatives can assist in connecting patients with appropriate local resources and assist people who face discrimination based on diabetes.

■ **American Heart Association**

www.americanheart.org

800.242.8721

Advocates for heart disease and stroke, the American Heart Association provides resources for patients, professionals, and the community through education and events. It also actively sponsors and raises funds for ongoing research.3. Other patient support services, such as

■ **Hospital Companions**

www.hospitalcompanions.com

877.502.6672

Hospital Companions aids patients and families during a hospitalization by providing nonmedical companionship and enhanced communication services. Patients have a Companion at their bedside who serves as a health advocate, working in cooperation with the medical staff. The patient's Companion develops a customized, web-accessible Patient Page™ that is used as a central place for concerned family and friends to visit and see how the patient is doing.

Conclusion: Patient Instruction Example

Congratulations on taking control of your healthcare! You have made a wise decision. After all, you are the best person to monitor your healthcare. As you use your PHP, do not think of it as a fixed record; rather, think of it as a fluid account of your healthcare experiences that grows and changes as you do. Do your best to keep current on your health conditions. This can be difficult in the midst of working, raising a family, and managing day-to-day life issues. My own experience taught me to practice what I preach. Upon receiving a call from my doctor's office about a past due bill, I almost made an immediate payment without questioning the charge. My conversation with the office assistant went something like this:

She said, "You owe $200, would you like to pay by credit card?" I responded, "Sure, but that sounds kind of high, did my insurance company pay anything?" She responded, "Yes, this is now your portion." That amount was much too high for a return office visit. So I asked,

"Can you tell me what CPT code I was charged for on that visit?" She responded with TWO procedure codes:

1. CPT code 99205 "Office or other outpatient visit" (new patient: typically 60 minutes)
2. CPT code 99213 "Established patient office or other outpatient visit" (typically 15 minutes)

I said, "First, I am not a new patient; second, I was only in the office for 10 minutes; and, finally, you can't bill me for two evaluation management codes." I asked that the bill be clarified and recoded. It ultimately was coded correctly and rebilled at a lower charge.

The goal of the patient advocate is to get the average person, even children, to talk "CPT language" and ask, "What exactly are you charging me for?" This is no different than going to the grocery store and being able to recognize each item purchased on the bill.

So get started! Just remember, if you find yourself stuck, hurt, or simply lost in the healthcare system or have run into a roadblock preventing you from receiving optimal care, do not despair—patient advocates are a great source of support!

Study Guide

1. Which of the following is one of the three steps to starting your PHP?
   a. Fill in your information to the best of your ability
   b. Schedule 20 minutes to start your PHP
   c. Take 5 minutes to gather all immediately available information
   d. All of the above
2. Which of the following should NOT be a section in your PHP?
   a. Emergency contacts
   b. Current medications
   c. Car insurance claims
   d. Allergies
3. Make a list of every healthcare provider you have seen, including
   a. Personal trainer
   b. Financial advisor
   c. Veterinarian
   d. None of the above
4. A (_____) will typically put you in contact with the medical records department or whoever manages the release of patient information.
   a. Insurance agent
   b. Nurse
   c. Hospital
   d. None of the above
5. If you have difficulties obtaining your information, who should you ask to speak with?
   a. Doctor
   b. Nurse
   c. Plan sponsor
   d. Provider's compliance officer

Answer Key:
   1. D   2. C   3. A   4. C   5. D

PATIENT ADVOCACY PHP TEMPLATES

Education breeds confidence. Confidence breeds hope. Hope breeds peace.

Confucius

This appendix contains the critical building blocks for a 360 degree perspective on an individual's health and welfare. A short introduction is provided, followed by several key templates.

- Personal Healthcare Portfolio (PHP) health: An overall picture of current health status, including key demographic information
- PHP wellness management: An overall picture of current wellness management programs, including self-recording assessments
- PHP financial management: Templates to begin tracking specific healthcare expenditures
- PHP personal health assessments: Template to track ongoing healthcare initiatives

Appendix I: Health

The secret of getting ahead is getting started.

Mark Twain

Introduction

Our healthcare system is complicated. Having your health information organized and accessible will enable you to simplify your healthcare experience. Medical Business Associates' Personal Healthcare Portfolio (PHP) has the ability to empower you to

1. Improve your healthcare experience
   a. To feel "more in control"
   b. To become a conscientious consumer of healthcare
   c. To feel hopeful about your health
2. Assemble your healthcare facts (clinical and financial)
   a. To manage and control your healthcare information
   b. To make informed decisions about your care
   c. To facilitate the best care possible
   d. To manage, control, and reduce your healthcare costs
   e. To prevent clinically adverse outcomes
   f. To guard your protected health information from fraud, waste, and abuse

Your PHP is private and confidential. You own your healthcare information and whatever content you put into your PHP. Federal laws such as the Health Information Portability and Accountability Act (HIPAA) protect the privacy of your health information. These laws protect your individually identifiable health information, whether it is maintained or transmitted in writing, electronically, or orally. Your individually identifiable health information includes information about your physical and mental health, the receipt and payment of your healthcare services, and your participation in your health plan.

You are not required to share your PHP with any organization or person that you do not completely trust. Your PHP may contain private information that you do not feel comfortable sharing. To ensure that your information is safe, take precautions with the storage of your PHP.

Health

Why is it important to track your health? That is simple. An accurate record of your health can save your life. This section begins by asking you about your basic personal information and then provides forms that will help you manage events related to your health.

Take a moment to reflect on the purpose of your PHP. The contents of your record are required by your healthcare providers to perform a comprehensive evaluation of your health status and to recommend treatment and wellness options that best reflect your health status. A healthcare provider is anyone (e.g., doctors, nurses, or pharmacists) who provides you with care to treat or prevent sickness, disease, ailments, and other healthcare issues.

How confident are you that your healthcare providers have all of your personal healthcare information at their fingertips? Perhaps someday, with the advancement of electronic records, healthcare providers will be able to retrieve and review your health history at the press of a button. In the meantime, it is important to arm yourself with your information. With your PHP in hand, you have access to your health information when you need it. By maintaining your PHP, you will be empowered to take charge of your health and make optimal decisions about your care.

Please contact Medical Business Associates for additional forms or support. Our patient advocates are here to navigate patients through the complex world of healthcare, answer patient questions, and help resolve patient concerns; help patients assemble, maintain, and use their personal health records; and help victims of medical and financial errors, fraud, waste, and abuse (e.g., medical identity theft).

Reminder Checklist

1. Before filling in this section, gather your personal records that you use for identification, such as your social security card, birth certificate, health insurance card, and driver's license or state identification.
2. If you cannot remember all of your healthcare providers from memory, review your past healthcare bills to collect your healthcare providers' names and contact information.
3. Contact your current healthcare providers to ask them to print you a list of all your bills for the past two years as well as a complete copy of your medical records. You can use the request forms in this appendix to help you. You

may want to ask for the same from important healthcare providers that have treated you in the past.

4. Include your medical advance directive. Advance directives are instructions you create that specify what actions need to be taken in the event that your health deteriorates to a point that you cannot advocate on behalf of yourself (e.g., a living will).

If you have any questions or need help to get started or maintain your PHP, contact a patient advocate at Medical Business Associates.

Contact Medical Business Associates
E-mail: patientadvocate@mbaaudit.com

PERSONAL

Please fill out the fields below. It is important to keep this information accurate and up to date.

PATIENT NAME AND ADDRESS

Prefix: _____

First Name: _____

Middle Name: _____

Last Name: _____

Suffix: _____

Address 1: _____

Address 2: _____

City: _____

State: _____

County: _____

Zip Code: _____

PATIENT INFO

Social Security #: _____   Languages Spoken: _____

Height: _____   Gender: _____

Weight: _____   Date of Birth: _____

Blood Type: _____   Birth City: _____

Ethnicity: _____   Birth Country: _____

Eye color: _____

CONTACT INFO

Home Phone: _____   Work Phone: _____

Cell Phone: _____   Fax: _____

E-Mail: _____

OCCUPATION AND MARITAL STATUS

Employment: _____   Marital Status: _____

Occupation: _____   Living with Spouse: _____

Highest Education Level: _____   Number of Dependents: _____

RELIGIOUS REQUIREMENTS AND NOTES

EMERGENCY CONTACTS: IN THE HOME (SPOUSE, ETC.)

Name: _____

Relationship: _____

Work Phone: _____

Home Phone: _____

Cell Phone: _____

Email: _____

EMERGENCY CONTACTS: OUTSIDE OF THE HOME (GROWN CHILD, SIBLING, ETC.)

Name: _____

Relationship: _____

Work Phone: _____

Home Phone: _____

Cell Phone: _____

Email: _____

EMERGENCY CONTACTS: OTHER

Name: _____

Relationship: _____

Work Phone: _____

Home Phone: _____

Cell Phone: _____

Email: _____

NOTES

PRIMARY HEALTHCARE PROVIDER

Please record your healthcare provider information here.

NAME

Prefix: _____

First Name: _____

Middle Name: _____

Last Name: _____

Suffix: _____

Address 1: _____

Address 2: _____

City: _____

State: _____

County: _____

Zip Code: _____

CONTACTS

Work Phone: _____

Home Phone: _____

Cell Phone: _____

Pager: _____

Fax: _____

Email: _____

SPECIALTY

Primary Care Physician: _____

or

Specialty

(P.T., Chiropractic,

acupuncture, cardiac,

orthopedic, etc.): _____

NOTES

SECONDARY HEALTHCARE PROVIDER

Please record your healthcare provider information here.

NAME

Prefix: _____

First Name: _____

Middle Name: _____

Last Name: _____

Suffix: _____

Address 1: _____

Address 2: _____

City: _____

State: _____

County: _____

Zip Code: _____

CONTACTS

Work Phone: _____

Home Phone: _____

Cell Phone: _____

Pager: _____

Fax: _____

Email: _____

SPECIALTY

Specialty (P.T., Chiropractic,
acupuncture, cardiac,
orthopedic, etc.): _____

NOTES

HEALTH INSURANCE

Please record your health insurance carrier information here.

PRIMARY

Insurance: _____

Group Number: _____

Policy Number: _____

Name of Insured: _____

Unique ID: _____

Currently Active: _____

Start Date: _____

End Date: _____

Type: _____

SECONDARY

Insurance: _____

Group Number: _____

Policy Number: _____

Name of Insured: _____

Unique ID: _____

Currently Active: _____

Start Date: _____

End Date: _____

Type: _____

NOTES

ACTIVE ILLNESS

Provide information relating to any current illnesses that you are experiencing now.

ILLNESS 1

List symptoms:

Beginning date of symptoms:	End date of symptoms:

Treatment:

Duration and effectiveness of treatment:

Was there a change in diet, vitamins, prescription medication, or environment preceding symptoms?

Diagnosis:

Treatment prescribed:

Risk/Side effects:

Results of treatment:

Date of follow-up visit:

Follow-up results:

ACTIVE ILLNESS

Provide information relating to any current illnesses that you are experiencing now.

ILLNESS 2

List symptoms:

Beginning date of symptoms:	End date of symptoms:

Treatment:

Duration and effectiveness of treatment:

Was there a change in diet, vitamins, prescription medication, or environment preceding symptoms?

Diagnosis:

Treatment prescribed:

Risk/Side effects:

Results of treatment:

Date of follow-up visit:

Follow-up results:

164

ACTIVE ILLNESS

Provide information relating to any current illnesses that you are experiencing now.

ILLNESS 3

List symptoms:

Beginning date of symptoms: | End date of symptoms:

Treatment:

Duration and effectiveness of treatment:

Was there a change in diet, vitamins, prescription medication, or environment preceding symptoms?

Diagnosis:

Treatment prescribed:

Risk/Side effects:

Results of treatment:

Date of follow-up visit:

Follow-up results:

ACTIVE ILLNESS

Provide information relating to any current illnesses that you are experiencing now.

ILLNESS 4

List symptoms:

Beginning date of symptoms:	End date of symptoms:

Treatment:

Duration and effectiveness of treatment:

Was there a change in diet, vitamins, prescription medication, or environment preceding symptoms?

Diagnosis:

Treatment prescribed:

Risk/Side effects:

Results of treatment:

Date of follow-up visit:

Follow-up results:

SURGERIES

Record a history of all of your surgeries here.

SURGERY RECORD

Have you ever had any type of surgery?	☐ Yes ☐ No

Please list dates and reasons for surgery

_____

_____

_____

_____

_____

_____

_____

_____

_____

_____

Do you require an antibiotic prophylaxis (an antibiotic taken prior to surgery to prevent an anticipated bacterial infection) prior to a surgical procedure?	☐ Yes ☐ No
Anesthesia (treatment with medicine that causes a loss of feeling) complications? (local anesthesia numbs only part of the body, general anesthesia causes loss of consciousness)	
Have you ever had any complications to anesthesia (heart problems, breathing problems, severe vomiting, high temperature, etc.)?	☐ Yes ☐ No

If yes, please explain:

_____

Has an immediate family member had complications with anesthesia?	☐ Yes ☐ No

If yes, please explain:

_____

_____

_____

_____

_____

_____

_____

CURRENT MEDICATION

Please list any medications that you currently take here. Include non-prescription medications (over the counter) and nutritional supplements such as vitamins. Please see next page for asthma medications.

Type (oral, injection, etc.)	Name	Dosage	Start	End	Reason for taking medication	Prescribed by	Instructions

ASTHMA MEDICATIONS

Record your asthma (chronic inflammation disease of the lungs) medications here.

ASTHMA MEDICATION RECORD

Do you currently take medications for asthma?

Name/Dosage   Frequency

_____

_____

_____

_____

_____

_____

_____

_____

NOTES

ALLERGIES

Record your allergy information here.

ALLERGY TYPE 1

Allergy to: _____

Reaction:

ALLERGIC REACTION INCIDENT 1 RELATED TO ALLERGY TYPE 1

Record allergic reaction incidents here.

Date	Cause

Was the allergy treated? _____

Who treated the allergy? _____

How was the allergy treated? _____

When was the allergy treated? _____

ALLERGIC REACTION INCIDENT 2 RELATED TO ALLERGY TYPE 1

Date	Cause

Was the allergy treated? _____

Who treated the allergy? _____

How was the allergy treated? _____

When was the allergy treated? _____

ALLERGIC REACTION INCIDENT 3 RELATED TO ALLERGY TYPE 1

Date	Cause

Was the allergy treated? _____

Who treated the allergy? _____

How was the allergy treated? _____

When was the allergy treated? _____

ALLERGIES

Record your allergy information here.

ALLERGY TYPE 2

Allergy to: _____

Reaction:

ALLERGIC REACTION INCIDENT 1 RELATED TO ALLERGY TYPE 2

Record allergic reaction incidents here.

Date	Cause

Was the allergy treated? _____

Who treated the allergy? _____

How was the allergy treated? _____

When was the allergy treated? _____

ALLERGIC REACTION INCIDENT 2 RELATED TO ALLERGY TYPE 2

Date	Cause

Was the allergy treated? _____

Who treated the allergy? _____

How was the allergy treated? _____

When was the allergy treated? _____

ALLERGIC REACTION INCIDENT 3 RELATED TO ALLERGY TYPE 2

Date	Cause

Was the allergy treated? _____

Who treated the allergy? _____

How was the allergy treated? _____

When was the allergy treated? _____

ALLERGIES

Record your allergy information here.

ALLERGY TYPE 3

Allergy to: _____

Reaction:

```
┌─────────────────────────────────────────────┐
│                                             │
│                                             │
│                                             │
│                                             │
│                                             │
│                                             │
│                                             │
│                                             │
│                                             │
│                                             │
│                                             │
│                                             │
└─────────────────────────────────────────────┘
```

ALLERGIC REACTION INCIDENT 1 RELATED TO ALLERGY TYPE 3

Record allergic reaction incidents here.

Date	Cause

Was the allergy treated? _____

Who treated the allergy? _____

How was the allergy treated? _____

When was the allergy treated? _____

ALLERGIC REACTION INCIDENT 2 RELATED TO ALLERGY TYPE 3

Date

Cause

Was the allergy treated? _____

Who treated the allergy? _____

How was the allergy treated? _____

When was the allergy treated? _____

ALLERGIC REACTION INCIDENT 3 RELATED TO ALLERGY TYPE 3

Date

Cause

Was the allergy treated? _____

Who treated the allergy? _____

How was the allergy treated? _____

When was the allergy treated? _____

Appendix II: Wellness Management

The more prepared I am, the more I'll be in control, less nervous, less stressed and more focused.

Marilu Henner
American actress

Wellness Management

People get involved with wellness programs to learn and develop good habits that help them live long, healthy lives. If this is not reason enough to get involved, many employers offer wellness programs to their employees (some with financial incentives) to control the rising costs of healthcare. Employers are looking out for the best interests of their employees—also recognizing that it is more cost-effective to keep employees healthy.

This section will help you manage your wellness programs, track your progress, and ultimately turn healthy behaviors into healthy habits. If you already participate in a wellness program, this section will help you organize all the plan information necessary to reach your wellness goals. If you do not currently participate in a wellness program, check with your employer for any wellness programs. Also, check with your healthcare providers to see if they recommend any specific wellness plans that you should follow independently.

Reminder Checklist

1. Review your healthcare records for any relevant historical information about any health issue that may require monitoring or treatment (now or in the future).
2. Whether you actively participate in a wellness program or are just beginning one, record information about your current status to benchmark your

progress against the goals that you set for yourself or with your healthcare providers.

3. Ask your healthcare providers whether a "health coach" can help you reach your goals.

4. If you are already participating in a wellness program (on your own or through your employer), collect all related documents and records and add them to the corresponding section in your Personal Healthcare Portfolio (PHP).

If you have any questions or need help to get started or maintain your PHP, contact a patient advocate at Medical Business Associates.

Contact Medical Business Associates
E-mail: patientadvocate@mbaaudit.com

ALCOHOL/DRUG ABUSE

Please record information related to your alcohol and drug usage here.

Do you smoke? ☐ Yes ☐ No
Details:

Do you drink alcohol? ☐ Yes ☐ No
Details (How many drinks per week?):

Do you use drugs such as heroin, crack, PCP, meth, marijuana?: ☐ Yes ☐ No
Details:

When was the last time you took these types of drugs?: _____
Details:

NOTES

CARDIOVASCULAR

Please record information related to your heart and blood vessels here.

Have you ever experienced the following?

Chest pain while walking or lying down? ☐ Yes ☐ No
Details:

Swelling in hands, feet or ankles: ☐ Yes ☐ No
Details:

Irregular heartbeat (heart flutters): ☐ Yes ☐ No
Details:

Varicose veins: ☐ Yes ☐ No
Details:

Shortness of breath: ☐ Yes ☐ No
Details:

Fatigue: ☐ Yes ☐ No
Details:

Sweating without exercise: ☐ Yes ☐ No
Details:

Upset stomach or stomach pain: ☐ Yes ☐ No
Details:

Decreased exercise tolerance: ☐ Yes ☐ No
Details:

Pain while walking: ☐ Yes ☐ No
Details:

CARDIOVASCULAR (continued)

Leg cramps: ☐ Yes ☐ No
Details:

Leg ulcers: ☐ Yes ☐ No
Details:

Pale or cold fingers/toes: ☐ Yes ☐ No
Details:

Brown coloration in ankles: ☐ Yes ☐ No
Details:

Cold Hands/Feet: ☐ Yes ☐ No
Details:

Other:
Details:

Other:
Details:

Other:
Details:

Other:
Details:

Other:
Details:

Other:
Details:

STRESS LEVEL

Please record information regarding your stress here. Rate your feelings of stress at the following places/situations using the number 0–10. 10 being the highest stress level.

Home

Work

Driving your automobile

Working on a hobby

Playing a sport

Visiting your family (not living in your home)

Traveling:

Other:

Other:

Other:

Other:

NOTES

WEIGHT

Record your weight and eating habit information here.

EATING HABITS

	Times per week that you eat	Time of day	Location (living room, kitchen table, work, etc.)
Breakfast			
Snack			
Lunch			
Snack			
Dinner			
Snack			

Daily Consumption (record number of beverages per day)

Coffee _____

Soft Drinks (nondiet) _____

Soft Drinks (sugar-free) _____

Tea _____

Water _____

Milk _____

Beer _____

Wine _____

Hard Liquor _____

WEIGHT ASSESSMENT

Record information about your weight here.

Have you ever had a problem managing your weight? _____

Can you recall any specific instance with the onset of your weight problem? _____

If so: list weight before and after onset of weight problem: BMI
BMI= Weight in pounds × 703 / Height in inches _____

If so: list your current BMI before and after onset of weight problem: Before: _____
After: _____

Has your weight fluctuated or been stable? _____

Have you tried to lose unwanted weight? _____

How many meals do you eat a day? _____

What is your daily calorie intake? _____

Does your weekend diet differ from your weekday diet? _____

Please rank the following attempts at losing weight
in order of effectiveness for you (0=haven't tried)

Lost weight on your own without professional	
Commercial weight loss programs	
Self-help groups	
Consultations with dietician	
Psychiatric help	
Personal trainer	
Liquid diet	
Medication	
Surgery	

EXERCISE

Record your usual weekly exercise behavior.

Weekday	Exercise / Sport	Level of intensity	Duration	Initial heart rate	End heart rate	Comments
Monday						
Tuesday						
Wednesday						
Thursday						
Friday						
Saturday						
Sunday						
Total						

Appendix III: Financial Documentation

Time is a currency you can only spend once, so be careful how you spend it.

Harmon Okinyo
artist, writer

Financial

Why is it important to track and plan for healthcare expenditures? Billing errors can cause you to pay more than you actually owe. Verifying prices before you spend your money will save out-of-pocket costs. Careful tracking of your expenses will help you manage your healthcare expenditures.

If you have insurance, this section is also helpful to track precertification quotes for healthcare services. Remember to review your explanation of benefits (EOB)—the "receipt" that your insurance company will send to you after you receive a healthcare service. EOBs are also referred to as explanation of reviews. EOBs may be confusing, but at minimum, review them and document them.

Reminder Checklist

1. Collect and file all EOBs that you receive from your insurance company and billing statements that you receive from your healthcare providers.
2. Log all "out-of-pocket" expenses (e.g., co-pays).
3. Remember that some healthcare expenditures may be written off against your tax return. Talk to a patient advocate or your accountant if you have questions about tax-exempt healthcare services.
4. Look at the healthcare services on your billing statements to confirm that you actually received the service listed and that you actually did visit the

provider listed on the bill.

5. If you receive a bill that does not belong to you, pick up the phone as soon as possible and call your healthcare provider and insurance company. You may be a victim of medical identity theft.

6. If you feel that your identity has been compromised, contact a health information specialist, the identity theft hotline for your state, and the provider to report a potential use of your identity. Someone else could be using your identity to receive healthcare services and/or monetary gain from those services.

If you have any questions or need help to get started or maintain your Personal Healthcare Portfolio (PHP), contact a patient advocate at Medical Business Associates.

Contact Medical Business Associates
E-mail: patientadvocate@mbaaudit.com

EXPLANATION OF BENEFITS

Record your co-pays and insurance payments here.

Date	Insurance Company	Co-pay	Benefits Received	Paid To	Date Expires

189

HEALTHCARE PROVIDER BILLING STATEMENTS

Record billing information here.

Date	Insurance Company	Service Rendered	Amount Billed	Amount Paid by Insurance	"Out-of-Pocket" Expense	Comments

HEALTHCARE PROVIDER QUOTES

Record quotes for services requested from your healthcare provider here.

Date	Test/Service	Healthcare Provider	Location	Price	Comments

MEDICATION QUOTES

Please record quotes for medication here.

Date	Medication	Healthcare Provider	Pharmacy	Price	Comments

Appendix IV: Personal Health Assessments

Your life is the sum result of all the choices you make, both consciously and unconsciously. If you can control the process of choosing, you can take control of all aspects of your life. You can find the freedom that comes from being in charge of yourself.

Robert F. Bennett
U.S. senator

Personal Health Assessments

Why is it important to complete and update personal health assessments? The answer is easy. By completing this section of your Personal Healthcare Portfolio (PHP), you and your healthcare providers will gain a clear understanding of your current health issues. The assessments in this section will also help to prioritize which issues require immediate attention and those that might be put off until a later date.

The assessments in this section will also help to determine appropriate actions for any pending lifestyle changes that your healthcare provider might have suggested. If you are not sure how to make needed lifestyle changes or need help getting started (or staying on track!), then contact a patient advocate. Utilizing a patient advocate can help you to achieve your health goals. Personal health coaches provide you with as much support as you need to reach your goals. A certified professional can help you change unhealthy behaviors, create new healthy habits, track your health status and progress, and stay on your new path to a healthy life—reducing the risk of disease and life-threatening conditions.

Reminder Checklist

1. Review your event log in the health section of your PHP to recall any significant health events to add to your personal health time line.
2. Contact your current healthcare providers for a copy of your bills and medical records if you have not yet done so.
3. Talk to family members to find out if they know of any genetic conditions or issues that might affect you.

If you have any questions or need help to get started or maintain your PHP, contact a patient advocate at Medical Business Associates.

Contact Medical Business Associates
E-mail: patientadvocate@mbaaudit.com

PERSONAL HEALTH TIMELINE

List any significant health events (including surgeries, symptom occurrences, hospitalizations, etc.) that have happened during your life:

Birth to Age 1: (Infancy)

Age 1 to 4 (Early Childhood):

Age 5 to 11 (Grade School):

Age 12 to 17 (Junior High and High School):

Age 18 to 23 (College, Early Adulthood):

Age 23 to 35 (Adulthood):

Age 36 to 50:

Age 51 to 60:

Age 61 to 70:

Age 71 to 80:

Age 81 and above:

ILLNESS HISTORY

Check off each of the following illnesses that you have experienced during your life. Provide related comments about the illnesses as appropriate. For example, "Treated for prostate cancer in 2007 . . . it is currently in remission."

Illness	Yes/No	Comments
Abnormal Heartbeat		
ADHD/ADD		
Alcoholism		
Alzheimer's		
Anemia		
Aneurism		
Anorexia/Bulimia		
Anxiety/Panic Attacks		
Arthritis		
Artificial Joints		
Asthma		
Autism		
Back Problems		
Bacterial Meningitis		
Bleeding Problems		
Blood Clots		
Blood Circulation Problems		
Blood Disease		
Cancer		
Canker Sores		
Cataracts		
Chemical Dependency		
Chemotherapy		
Chest Pain/Pressure		
Chicken Pox		

ILLNESS HISTORY (continued)

Illness	Yes/No	Comments
Chlamydia		
Crohn's Disease		
Colitis		
Congenital Heart Disease		
Corneal Abrasions		
Dementia		
Dental Problems		
Dentures		
Depression		
Diabetes		
Diabetic Complications		
Diverticulitis		
Dizziness		
Drug Dependency		
Ear Infection		
Eczema		
Emphysema		
Epilepsy		
Eye Problems		
Fainting		
Fibromyalgia		
Gallbladder Disease		
Genital Warts		
Glaucoma		
Glasses or Contacts		
Gonorrhea		
Gout		

ILLNESS HISTORY (continued)

Illness	Yes/No	Comments
Handicaps/Disabilities		
Hair Loss		
Headaches/Migraines		
Illness Yes/No Comments		
Hearing Problems		
Heart Attack		
Heart Problems		
Heart Murmur		
Hemodialysis		
Hepatitis		
Herpes Simplex		
High Blood Pressure		
High Blood Sugar		
HIV/AIDS		
High Cholesterol		
High Triglycerides		
Infertility		
Intestinal Problems		
Irritable Bowel Syndrome		
Jaundice		
Joint Problems		
Kidney Problems		
Kidney Stones		
Liver Problems		
Low Blood Pressure		
Low Blood Sugar		
Lung Problems		

ILLNESS HISTORY (continued)

Illness	Yes/No	Comments
Lupus		
Lyme Disease		
Malignant Hyperthermia		
Measles		
Mental Retardation		
Mitral Valve Prolapse		
Mononucleosis		
Multiple Sclerosis		
Mumps		
Muscular Dystrophy		
Neck Problems		
Neurological Problems		
Nose Bleeds		
Open Wounds		
Osteoporosis		
Osteopenia		
Pacemaker		
Paralysis		
Parkinson's Disease		
Pelvic/Vaginal Infections		
Pertussis/Whooping Cough		
Pleurisy		
Phlebitis		
Pink Eye		
Pneumonia		
Polio		
Prostate Problems		

ILLNESS HISTORY (continued)

Illness	Yes/No	Comments
Prosthesis		
Psoriasis		
Pulmonary Embolism		
Radiation Treatment		
Rectal Bleeding/Hemorrhoids		
Respiratory Infections		
Rheumatism		
Rheumatic Fever		
Rubella		
Scabies		
Scarlet Fever		
Seizures		
Sexual Dysfunction		
Shingles		
Sickle Cell Disease		
Shortness of Breath		
Sinus Infection		
Skin Disease		
Sleep Apnea		
Speech Problems		
Strep Throat		
Stomach Problems/Reflux		
Strokes/CVA		
Syphilis		
Thyroid Problems		
Tonsillitis		

ILLNESS HISTORY (continued)

Illness	Yes/No	Comments
Tuberculosis		
Tumors		
Ulcers		
Urinary Tract Infections		
Vision Problems		
Viral Meningitis		
Warts		
Other		
Other		
Other		
Other		
Other		
Other		
Other		
Other		
Other		
Other		
Other		
Other		
Other		
Other		
Other		
Other		
Other		
Other		
Other		
Other		

GENETIC HISTORY

If available, record your family history in the following sections. Knowing the health history of your ancestors can keep you alert to any warning signs and lead to early detection which can save your life.

PRENATAL

Name of Your Father: _____

Date of Birth: _____

Ethnicity: _____

Religion: _____

Occupation: _____

Name of Your Mother: _____

Date of Birth: _____

Ethnicity: _____

Religion: _____

Occupation: _____

Your Mother's Pregnancy History

Pregnancy duration (wks): _____

Your Mother's Age: _____

Your Father's Age: _____

Complication:

Exposures (Something your mother might have been exposed to): _____

Your Birth History

Location (Hospital, Home): _____

Mode (Vaginal, C-Section): _____

Birth Weight: _____

Birth Height: _____

Birth Complications:

GENETIC HISTORY (continued)

If available, record your childhood milestones here.

PEDIATRIC

Your Developmental History Record your age in months.

Smiled: _____

Rolled over: _____

Sat with support: _____

Held own head up: _____

First word: _____

Reached for objects: _____

Sat up: _____

Crawled: _____

Walked: _____

Growth History

Significant past medical history: _____

_____

_____

_____

_____

_____

_____

_____

_____

Describe any medical health issues that occurred during childhood (i.e., asthma, allergies, seizures):

FAMILY HISTORY

Provide information related to your family history here.

Name:

Unknown due to Adoption: [   ]
Unknown due to Other: [   ]

Biological Family Member	Living (Year Born)	Deceased (Age at/Cause of Death)
Grandfather		
Grandfather		
Grandmother		
Grandmother		
Father		
Mother		
Brother ☐ Sister ☐ Full ☐ Half ☐		
Brother ☐ Sister ☐ Full ☐ Half ☐		
Brother ☐ Sister ☐ Full ☐ Half ☐		
Brother ☐ Sister ☐ Full ☐ Half ☐		
Brother ☐ Sister ☐ Full ☐ Half ☐		
Brother ☐ Sister ☐ Full ☐ Half ☐		
Brother ☐ Sister ☐ Full ☐ Half ☐		
Brother ☐ Sister ☐ Full ☐ Half ☐		
Brother ☐ Sister ☐ Full ☐ Half ☐		
Brother ☐ Sister ☐ Full ☐ Half ☐		
Son ☐ Daughter ☐		
Son ☐ Daughter ☐		
Son ☐ Daughter ☐		
Son ☐ Daughter ☐		
Son ☐ Daughter ☐		
Son ☐ Daughter ☐		
Son ☐ Daughter ☐		
Son ☐ Daughter ☐		
Son ☐ Daughter ☐		
Son ☐ Daughter ☐		

Family History (continued)

In general, how much of a problem do you think your family members and loved ones have with the following? (Please list initials of family members that fit into the following categories)	No Problem	Somewhat of a Problem	Significant Problem
Getting into trouble			
Getting along with his or her mother			
Getting along with his or her father			
Feeling happy or sad			
His or her behavior at school			
Having fun			
Getting along with adults other than parents			
Feeling nervous			
Getting along with siblings			
Getting along with peers			
Getting involved in activities			
Schoolwork			
Behavior at home			
Interruption of personal time			
Disruption of family routines			
Any family member having to do without things			
Any family member to suffer negative mental or physical health			
Financial strain on your family			
Less attention to be paid to other children			
Disruption or upset of relationship within the family			
Disruption of your family's social activities			
You miss work or neglect other duties			

Family History (continued)

Have any of your blood relatives had any of the following:	Family Member
Allergy—Food: Details:	
Allergy—Medications: Details:	
Alcoholism: Details:	
Alzheimer's Disease: Details:	
Arthritis: Details:	
ADHD/ADD: Details:	
Autism: Details:	
Bleeding Problems: Details:	
Birth Problems (unusual size, color, etc.): Details:	
Bone Problems: Details:	

Family History (continued)

Have any of your blood relatives had any of the following:	Family Member
Cancer: Details:	
Cardiovascular Disease: Details:	
Cerebral Palsy: Details:	
Cleft Lip/Palate: Details:	
Club Foot: Details:	
Convulsions/Seizures: Details:	
Cystic Fibrosis: Details:	
Emotional Problems: Details:	
Diabetes (Type I or II): Details:	
Down Syndrome: Details:	
Dwarfism: Details:	
Drug Addiction: Details:	

Family History (continued)

Have any of your blood relatives had any of the following:	Family Member
Foot Abnormalities (extra/missing toes, webbed, etc.): Details:	
Gastrointestinal Disease: Details:	
Gout: Details:	
Hand Abnormalities (extra/missing fingers, webbed, etc.): Details:	
Headaches/Migraines: Details:	
Hearing Problems: Details:	
Heart Problems: Details:	
Hepatitis: Details:	
Hernia: Details	
High Blood Pressure: Details:	
High Cholesterol or High Triglycerides: Details:	
Hormone Problems: Details:	

Family History (continued)

Have any of your blood relatives had any of the following:	Family Member
HIV/AIDS: Details:	
Huntington's Disease: Details:	
Hydrocephalus: Details:	
Joint Problems: Details:	
Infertility: Details:	
Kidney Disease: Details:	
Learning Disabilities: Details:	
Liver Disease: Details:	
Lou Gehrig's Disease: Details:	
Lung Problems: Details:	

Family History (continued)

Have any of your blood relatives had any of the following:	Family Member
Lupus: Details:	
Miscarriages: Details:	
Mental Illness: Details:	
Mental Retardation: Details:	
Multiple Births: Details:	
Multiple Sclerosis: Details:	
Muscular Dystrophy: Details:	
Muscle Weakness: Details:	
Myasthenia Gravis: Details:	
Parkinson's Disease: Details:	
Patches of Hair/Skin Discoloration: Details:	

Family History (continued)

Have any of your blood relatives had any of the following:	Family Member
Phenylketonuria: Details:	
Scoliosis: Details:	
Skin Problems: Details:	
Rh Disease: Details:	
Sickle Cell Disease: Details:	
Special Education: Details:	
Speech Problems: Details:	
Spina Bifida (open spine): Details:	
Stroke: Details:	
Stomach Problems: Details:	
Stillbirths: Details:	
Suicide: Details:	

Family History (continued)

Have any of your blood relatives had any of the following:	Family Member
Tay-Sachs Disease: Details:	
Thalessemia: Details:	
Thyroid Disease: Details:	
Tuberculosis: Details:	
Sight Problems: Details:	
Weight Problems: Details:	
Other Details: Details:	
Other Details: Details:	
Other Details: Details:	
Other Details: Details:	
Other Details: Details:	
Other Details: Details:	

Family History (continued)

How much have your child's problems caused:	No Problem	Somewhat a Problem	Big Problem
Interruption of personal time			
Disruption of family routines			
Any family member having to do without things			
Any family member to suffer negative mental or physical health			
Financial strain on your family			
Less attention to be paid to other children			
Disruption or upset of relationship within the family			
Disruption of your family's social activities			
You to miss work or neglect other duties			

Index